visual
communication

visual
communication

Understanding Maps, Charts, Diagrams, and Schematics

Ned Racine

NEW YORK

Library of Congress Cataloging-in-Publication Data:
Racine, Ned.
    Visual communication: understanding maps, charts, diagrams, and schematics/by Ned Racine—1st ed.
        p.cm.
Includes bibliographical references.
    ISBN 1-57685-393-4 (alk. paper)
    1. Visual communication. I. Title.

    P93.5 .R33 2002
    302.23—dc21

                                                2001050433

Printed in the United States of America

9 8 7 6 5 4 3 2 1

First Edition

ISBN 1-57685-393-4

For more information or to place an order, contact LearningExpress at:
    900 Broadway
    Suite 604
    New York, NY 10003

Or visit us at:
    www.learnatest.com

All images and references to Palm, Inc. or any of its products is with the permission of Palm, Inc. Palm™ is a trademark of Palm, Inc.

Palm, Inc. is not a sponsor of, or affiliated with, publication.

All images or screen captures of Windows, Excel, or PowerPoint programs found within this publication are courtesy of Microsoft Corp. Microsoft and/or its respective suppliers make no representations about the suitability of the information contained in the documents and related graphics published as part of the services for any purpose. All such documents and related graphics are provided "as is" without warranty of any kind. Microsoft and/or its respective suppliers hereby disclaim all warranties and conditions with regard to this information, including all warranties and conditions of merchantability, whether express, implied or statutory, fitness for a particular purpose, title and non-infringement. In no event shall Microsoft and/or its respective suppliers be liable for any special, indirect or consequential damages or any damages whatsoever resulting from loss of use, data or profits, whether in an action of contract, negligence or other tortious action, arising out of or in connection with the use or performance of information available from the services.

The documents and related graphics published on the services could include technical inaccuracies or typographical errors. Changes are periodically added to the information herein. Microsoft and/or its respective suppliers may make improvements and/or changes in the product(s) and/or the program(s) described herein at any time.

about the author

Ned Racine is a technical writer and consultant specializing in document design, graphic design, and presentation development. He is the author of the Peter Norton Series texts for *Microsoft Office* and *Power Point*. He lives in Altadena, California.

contents

▶ **four**

Tracking Information   61

▶ **five**

Explaining Data   81

▶ **six**

Solving Problems and Tracking Projects   109

Technical Drawings: Blueprints, Whiteprints, and Drawings 135

eight

From Circuits to Theaters: Using Schematics 159

Navigating the Computer World 177

visual
communication

Spatial/Visual Intelligence

why visual communication matters

The person who uses yesterday's tools in today's work won't be in business tomorrow.

—ANONYMOUS

JESSE was bright—everyone who met him thought so. Why he struggled in school remained a mystery to his parents. Jesse was someone who could explain computer animation in ways even parents could understand. By the time he was a sophomore in high school, he was working part-time for a company that created television commercials. Jesse designed some of their high-tech computer animation. Some of his animation even ended up in motion pictures.

By his senior year in high school, Jesse's brainpower and talents had made him enough money to buy himself a new car. However, his grades were still stuck at "C."

Jesse now attends the Rochester Institute of Technology, where he has just begun a new major, Computer Game Interface Design, a major created, in part, for him. You may ask, "With his unimpressive grade point average and tepid SAT scores, how did Jesse ever get in to such a high-powered technical college?" The truth is the R.I.T. admissions interviewers had met enough creative thinkers to recognize that Jesse is primarily a *visual/spatial learner*. He doesn't do as well listening, reading, and repeating (the teaching style that much of our institutional education is based upon). Jesse, however, does excel at:

- Absorbing everything visual
- Interpreting graphics and learning from them
- Creating visual answers to the questions his imagination poses

Jesse was (once discovered) mainly one kind of learner. Most people are a mixture of learning types.

Visual communication was the best way to reach Jesse. More than that, Jesse's true story suggests visual communication's power to support a range of learning styles. *Visual Communication* teaches how you can incorporate visual communication in your life and the life of your organization. After all, there are millions of Jesses out there. They are your classmates, coworkers, your investors, and your customers.

Visual communication—receiving and transmitting messages through visual means—reached Jesse when other forms of communication failed. If only for its power to reach a variety of learners, visual communication would be worth understanding.

There are, however, many more reasons to explore visual communication. Visual communication surrounds us. It helps us navigate the computer world or an interstate highway. It organizes information on the sports page of a newspaper or the maintenance manual of a nuclear reactor. And, as businesses strive to win customers around the world, visual communication carries their message, usually more clearly than words. In the 21st century, when *too much information* seems more of a problem than *not enough information*, visual communication offers a language to clarify and compress that information.

To help you *speak* the language of visual communication, this book has two goals:

- To teach you how to become a better consumer of visual communication.
- To teach you how to become a better creator of visual communication.

Of course, you might be a consumer of visual communication one day and a creator the next. And if you do not currently produce visual communication, you likely will during the course of your career. If you currently create visual communication, you can explore a broad range of visual communication forms, perhaps some you have never used, and better understand what makes effective visual communication effective.

Visual/spatial intelligence is one of eight intelligences defined by Howard Gardner in his research at Harvard University. Gardner says individuals may have one best way of learning or several types of intelligences that are more developed than others, leading to a variety of ways of absorbing information.

You will see *graphics* mentioned often in this book. **Graphics** are defined as visual and artistic representation, such as charts, drawings, icons, maps, and tables.

reaching those who are visual/spatial learners

THOSE WITH SPATIAL intelligence have the ability to:

- Perceive the complexity of a form or object
- Mentally manipulate a form or object, including rotating the form or object to reveal each side
- Create visual/spatial representations of their environment
- Create a graphic likeness of an actual object
- Transfer those representations either mentally or concretely

Visual/spatial learners, for example, sometimes nicknamed **visualizers**, often enjoy the following:

How do you recognize a visual/spatial learner? When handed an instructional manual, these workers turn first to the graphs, charts, and diagrams. When taking notes in a meeting, these visualizers draw complex patterns around their notes.

- Drawing
- Disassembling devices
- Building things
- Solving puzzles
- Doodling
- Grasping detail
- Relating parts to a whole
- Recalling locations by description or image
- Interpreting maps

Visual/spatial learners, for example, excel at the mental manipulation of forms and shapes. Figure 1-1 shows a box and how a visual/spatial learner might unfold and manipulate the box to reveal its sides.

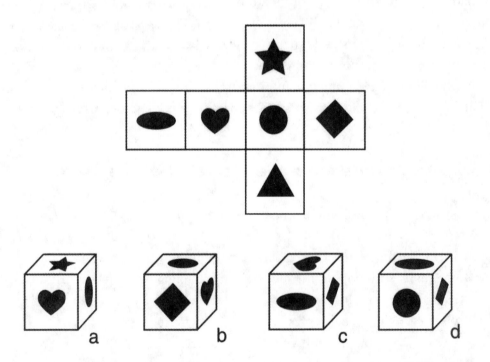

Figure 1-1: Visual/spatial learners excel at mentally manipulating forms and shapes

Visual/spatial learners tend to be more sophisticated in perceiving visual communication. Therefore, visual/spatial learners are valuable to organizations because these learners often become:

- Architects
- Engineers
- Draftspersons
- Graphic designers
- Mechanics
- Surveyors
- Urban planners

Frankly, an organization risks losing the talents and ideas of visual/spatial staff members, unless their primary method of learning is incorporated into the organization's communication. Few organizations have such a surplus of talent and ideas to justify ignoring visual/spatial staff members.

an old new tool

LATER IN CHAPTER 1, advantages of visual communication—offered to organizations in the 21st century—will be considered. This is not to say that visual communication is a new tool, even within North American society. Native Americans have long communicated with sign languages to bridge tribal barriers. The forms of sign language used by the deaf—studied by the nondeaf since the 1770s—culminated in today's rich and evocative sign languages, which each have their own syntax and grammar (e.g., American Sign Language).

Because we can interpret nonverbal communication, such as frowns, smiles, crossed arms, and shrugs, it can be said that we have **visual intelligence**. Visual intelligence includes the capacity to understand sign language, facial and body gestures, and graphics.

Human beings absorb many forms of visual communication, including:

- Cartoons
- Comic books
- Motion pictures
- Photography

- Posters
- Puppetry
- Sign language
- Slides
- Television

As you may gather from this chapter—and, in fact, from this entire book—visual communication contributes to **literacy**, the understanding and interpreting of information.

Visual communication is actually about applying what you read and see to accomplish a goal. Successful communication means you have received a message, and the results might be:

- Learning something new
- Responding with more or other information
- Taking some kind of action
- Storing the information for future use

Studies find that people who have trouble absorbing benefit from reading text interspersed with compelling graphics. In addition, learning to interpret charts, icons, symbols, tables, and maps stimulates the ability to summarize, compare and contrast, and problem-solve—all skills essential to reading well.

Widespread illiteracy is not a problem from another age or another country. Figure 1-2 presents several humbling facts about literacy in the United States:

These people . . .	. . . do this:
20% of American adults . . .	. . . read at or below the fifth-grade level (far below the level needed to earn a living wage)
40 million Americans age 16 and older . . .	. . . have significant literacy needs.
43% of people with the lowest literacy rates . . .	. . . live in poverty

These people . . .	. . . do this:
Workers who lack a high school diploma . . .	. . . earn an average monthly income of $452.
Workers with a college degree . . .	. . . earn an average monthly income of $1,829.

Figure 1-2: Visual communication benefits poor readers
Source: Data provided by Humboldt County (CA) Literacy Project, 2001.

Visual literacy is the ability to interpret the visible action, objects, or symbols found in the environment. In this book, visual literacy comes in two varieties:

1. Absorbing, understanding, and applying graphics. (What does this map show? Is this the map I need? Does this table help me understand my company's cash flow?)
2. Transforming information and goals into compelling graphics. (What type of chart illustrates what I want to say? Which icon explains best what I want to say?)

This book concentrates on designed or drawn visual communication, particularly those images distributed via paper and computer monitors. Within the world of those images, *Visual Communication* further focuses on the skills necessary to interpret or create visual communication, valuable talents in the 21st century business world. Consequently, you will be exposed to many forms of visual communication:

- Blueprints (and whiteprints)
- Charts
- Controls
- Diagrams
- Drawings
- Floorplans
- Globes
- Icons
- Presentations
- Schematics
- Signs
- Site plans
- Spreadsheets
- Symbols
- Tables
- Timelines

the most ancient communication

MOST ANTHROPOLOGISTS BELIEVE that mankind communicated with gestures and signing before communicating with sounds—in other words, visual communication preceded oral communication. These anthropologists theorize that early mankind reenacted events and told stories with gestures before the development of speech and drawing. Next, drawing became a tool to represent natural objects (e.g., cave drawings of animals) and stories (cave drawings of hunting, tribal movement, etc.), perhaps blossoming at the same time as spoken language.

Egyptian hieroglyphs and Chinese ideograms represent two later civilizations' efforts to develop written symbols to imitate body language signs and to express ideas. Figure 1-3 displays a result of those early, successful efforts, a Chinese ideogram for water.

Figure 1-3: The Chinese ideogram representing water

isn't this all automatic?

SEEING SOMETHING MIGHT be automatic—your eyes are open and you are facing in the right direction. *Perceiving* what you have seen is anything but automatic. Marlana Coe, in her book *Human Factors for Technical Communications*, describes the process of interpreting visual information as a series of steps. At one end of the series is sensation. At the other end is perception. **Sensation** means *receiving* impressions through hearing, seeing, smelling, and so forth. **Perception** means mentally *grasping* impressions gathered through the senses or understanding them.

For instance, two individuals might see the same event at the same instant, but one individual might grasp the meaning of the event faster and more completely. That individual would be more perceptive, her processes of interpreting sensation more sophisticated. Figure 1-4 maps the steps required to translate the sensation of a traffic sign to the perception of a traffic sign.

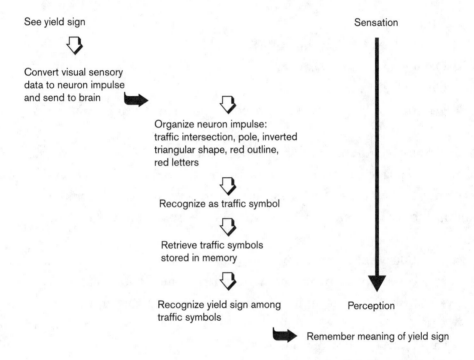

Figure 1-4: Our senses gather impressions and our brain translates them

Want to raise your visual/spatial IQ? Try these exercises:

- Identify a form from different angles or when "unfolded."
- Draw while looking at an object.
- Practice origami or the art of paper folding.
- Sculpt a 3-D clay version of a picture of an object.

advantages to communicating visually

Thinking is visual.

–SWISS EDUCATOR JOHANN HEINRICH PESTOLOZZI, 1746–1827

WHY TAKE THE time to create a piece of visual communication?

Frequently, visual communication represents the best opportunity to communicate with the widest range of people. The information that absolutely, positively must be communicated effectively is usually communicated visually:

- Road and traffic signs
- Building evacuation directions
- Danger and caution warnings
- Control labeling
- Location of basic services at airports, bus stations, and train stations

For example, Figure 1-5 displays an instruction sheet telling passengers how to leave a damaged airplane. How many words does the instruction sheet use?

Communicating visually has distinct advantages, as you will explore throughout this book. Here are several advantages of visual communication:

- Creating visual communication calls for summarizing information for easy consumption by readers and audiences, which often presents the person creating the communication with new insights and understanding.
- Visual communication addresses the need for global communication of basic but key information.
- Visual communication tends to be easier for other cultures to translate than text.
- If done correctly, visual communication resists misinterpretation.
- Visual communication allows teambuilding with others unfamiliar with the intricacies of your work.

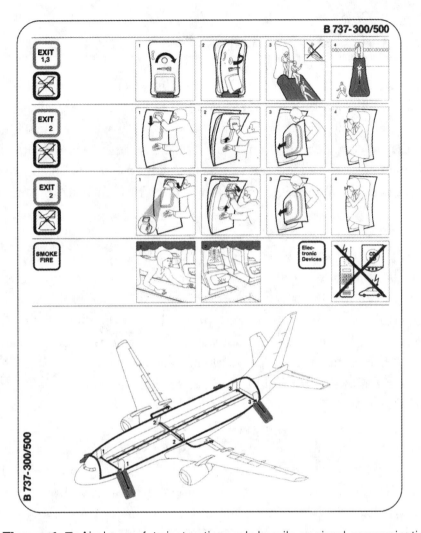

Figure 1-5: Airplane safety instructions rely heavily on visual communication

You need to look no further than the World Wide Web to see the value of visual communication in the 21st century. Fewer than ten years ago, users accessing information via online bulletin boards saw nothing but text on their computer screens. Can you remember the last text-only website you visited? What brought about this revolution?

keeping visual communication on track

BEFORE YOU ARE ready to communicate visually, you need to ask yourself several fundamental questions. Without finding complete and practical answers to these questions, your visual communication will be flawed and may confuse your audience. Practice answering these challenging questions with every graphic you design or assign. Soon you will recall these questions naturally. And remember that not all messages are best delivered through visual communication.

- *What is the goal of your visual communication?* (To inform your audience? To reassure stockholders? To explain factory expansion to employees?)

  If you pinpoint your goal, you are more likely to produce a simple piece of communication. As you proceed through other chapters, you will notice that the best works of visual communication are the most direct. There is beauty to an effective line chart or special map. Setting your goal and following it brings you closer to that simplicity.

- *What form best communicates your goal?* (A technical drawing? An icon? A map?)

  For example, suppose you want to show your machinists a technical drawing of a new wood screw your company will begin producing. How many views do you want in the drawing? In what scale do you want to show the screw? Is the screw one of an assembly of parts? Do you want to show the entire assembly? Figure 1-6 shows some of the views required to manufacture even a simple mechanical object.

Figure 1-6: Even a simple mechanical object such as a screw requires multiple views for accurate reproduction

As a consumer of visual communication, you experience the range of possibilities, even within a single form of visual communication. For example, photographs can be deeply moving, symbolic, or extremely realistic. Which kind do you want?

■ *Where should you place the visual communication?* (Above the signs at eye level? At the appropriate height for a person sitting in a wheelchair?)

On a sheet of paper within a report, letter, instruction manual, and so forth, pieces of visual communication should be clearly linked to the text they are illuminating. However, much of the visual communication we absorb does not appear in publications.

■ *What do you want your audience to do?* (Improve the quality of your company's products? Spend less time delivering parcels? Contribute ideas toward the new software product?)

■ *How do you want your audience to feel?* (Concerned? Amused? Proud? Involved?) Touching your audience's emotions becomes particularly important when giving presentations, as detailed in Chapter 10.

> Don't be afraid to use a piece of paper and a pen to create a draft of your communication, even before you turn on the computer. Many creators of visual communication believe their imagination flows best when completely unrestricted by the concerns of translating ideas into a computer application.

Effective visual communication demands the same attention to detail as effective writing. In fact, when creating visual communication for other societies—common in this age of globalized markets and international production teams—graphics must meet a higher standard of simplicity, clarity, and conciseness than text. This is because audiences from other cultures cannot rely on the context and elaboration found in written communication.

offering hope in the "too much information age"

The most striking paradox of the information age is this: The more information we produce, the less time we have to assimilate it.

—ROBERT L. LINDSTROM, AUTHOR OF THE *BUSINESS WEEK GUIDE TO MULTIMEDIA PRESENTATIONS*

PIECES OF VISUAL communication are often less ambiguous than words and often less prone to misinterpretation. Graphics make skimming easier and act as dividers to separate sections of a Web page. Graphics grab a viewer's attention. They emphasize major points and act as a guide in helping the viewer through the information.

Efforts to improve quality control and customer service—common goals for businesses in an age of international competition for markets and profits—require contributions from many people, all with different learning and working styles. Innovation, the life blood of high-tech companies, demands the ideas and insights from a variety of workers, all of whom cannot be reached by the same form of communication.

gLOSSARY

graphics—visual and artistic representation, such as charts, drawings, icons, maps, and tables

literacy—the understanding and interpreting of information

perception—mentally grasping impressions gathered through the senses

sensation—receiving impressions through hearing, seeing, smelling, tasting, and touching

visual communication—receiving and transmitting messages through visual means

visual intelligence—an ability to interpret nonverbal communication

visual literacy—the ability to interpret the visible action, objects, or symbols found in the environment

visual/spatial learner—an individual who best absorbs knowledge through viewing and creating graphics and other visual media

ten reasons why visual communication matters

1. Visual communication is less susceptible to misinterpretation than words.

2. Graphics can simplify and communicate complex ideas and data.

3. Visual aids add variety to text pages.

4. Visual representation can concisely demonstrate relationships.

5. Visual communication can spur the imagination and encourage brainstorming.

6. Visual symbols and icons are quickly and easily recognized.

7. Using texture, form, line, color, beauty, and mystery, compelling visual communication draws in the reader or audience.

8. Graphics can offer the manipulation of information within several forms (e.g., from data to *Excel* chart).

9. Your reader, or some of your audience, may be primarily or secondarily visual/spatial learners–that's how they best absorb information.

10. Visual representation allows for a holistic understanding that words alone cannot convey.

▶▶▶ learning on your own

1. Consider this: Why should businesses care that there are different kinds of learners?
2. What kinds of graphics—in, for example, textbooks, newspapers, magazines—do you generally find appealing? Why do think they are appealing to you?
3. Do an Internet or library search to find Gardner's eight learning styles. Which learning styles (besides visual/spatial) might lend themselves to the use of graphics and why? Is there a learning style that describes you?

Visual Communication in Everyday Life and Business

each day visual communication bombards us. Highway billboards use strong graphics to send a message before motorists drive out of reach. Television sports producers flash tables and charts on the screen so viewers can absorb information at a glance and quickly return to the game. Home appliances display symbols—not words—to explain the different positions of a switch or dial. With few or no words, road signs warn us when to stop or when we must yield to oncoming traffic.

As a daily consumer of visual communication, you are already an expert in translating visual communication

▶ **Signage**
▶ **Controls**
▶ **Gauges**
▶ **Diagrams**
▶ **Maps**
▶ **Tables**
▶ **Charts**

into ideas and directions. To strengthen your expert skills, this chapter offers an overview of forms of visual communication you may not have explored or considered.

signage

TRAFFIC SIGNS GUIDE automobiles, bicycles, buses, and motorcycles through cities around the world. They direct pilots from runway to terminal. Warning signs mark electrical cables and hazardous substances. Electronic signs display the arrival times of trains, then change to display the location of rental car agencies. The name for all this visual communication is **signage**.

Like all modern visual communication, signage must fight through a jungle of competing sights and sounds to grab a viewer's attention. Signage offers explanations, directions, and information. It must be clear and easily translated, while representing complex buildings, cities, and transit systems. How does a designer create easy-to-use signage when so much information must be communicated?

To meet these challenges, designers consider size, type style, colors, and where signage should be placed. To help users find information quickly, designers create a single look for signs within a building—for example, signage within an airport having large white letters on a blue background.

Effective signage can become a life-or-death issue. In April 1996, a fire at Düsseldorf Airport in Germany resulted in deaths and injuries. After the fire, a spokesperson for the city's fire brigade blamed the high number of causalities on passengers who ignored the emergency exit signs. Before Düsseldorf Airport reopened, airport management hired a design company to create a new set of powerful signage.

Figure 2-1 shows a range of modern signage.

Figure 2-1: A range of signage

controls

YOU USE CONTROLS every day—to turn on an electric fan, increase the volume on a television, or adjust the time of a clock. A **control** can be a switch, dial, wheel, button, knob, toggle, rod, or key.

With manufacturers targeting customers in multiple countries—speaking multiple languages—designers have changed controls to display fewer words and more universal symbols. In that way controls are prime examples of visual communication. But whether they use words or symbols, controls must meet several goals to be successful graphics.

- They should be clearly marked.
- They should be easy to remember.
- They should be easy to explain.

Figure 2-2 displays a dial that adjusts the speed of an electric fan. The lower ball indicates the current speed of the fan. When the ball lies directly under the first symbol on the left, the fan is off.

What do you think the other symbols mean?

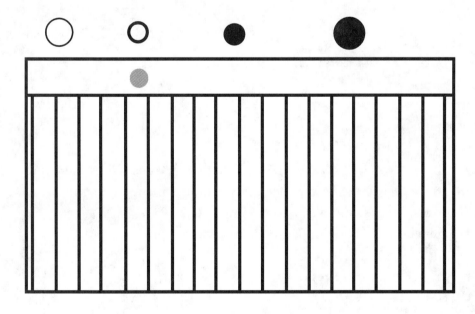

Figure 2-2: Control without words

Not every control can express its function without words. Sometimes text is required to avoid confusion, especially if a group of controls looks similar. Figure 2-3 contains a control commonly seen on video devices. In this example, symbols and text combine for clear communication.

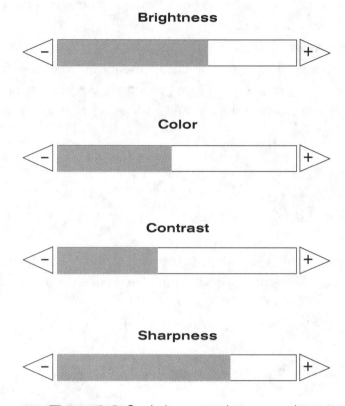

Figure 2-3: Symbols are not always enough

gauges

WHILE CONTROLS ALLOW us to adjust things, **gauges** tell us the condition of things. Gauges show how devices are operating in engines, computers, human organs, stereos, and wires, for example.

Gauges also tell us how much remains of something, as in:

- Air in automobile tires
- Power in a battery
- Film in a camera
- Gasoline and oil in a boat

Figure 2-4 displays this type of gauge: A gauge showing how much fuel remains in a tank. Typical of many gauges, this gauge has a pointing device (an arrow, needle, or line) that indicates current status. The viewer compares the needle with the lines showing the tank's capacity. These lines are often **tick marks**. The gauge in Figure 2-4 communicates that the tank is almost full.

This type of gauge often has a symbol to warn when a substance runs low. In this case, when the indicator line falls to the dark block at the bottom of the gauge, the user knows fuel is very low. Some fuel gauges may set off a low-fuel warning light.

Notice that a fuel gauge is so familiar to drivers that its creators do not mention fuel or gasoline or gallons; even full is abbreviated (F).

As you learn more about graphics, you will better understand how to create or select them. Although you cannot expect each graphic you use to be as familiar to your audience as a fuel gauge, you can learn lessons from Figure 2-4. When you begin creating or selecting graphics, keep these suggestions in mind:

■ Consider what your audience knows
■ Avoid explaining what they know
■ Focus on the essential information

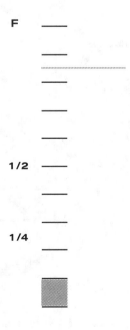

Figure 2-4: A common gauge

diagrams

DIAGRAMS ARE GRAPHICS that explain how something works or how it should be constructed or repaired. Diagrams can be sketches or plans. Common diagrams include blueprints (or the more popular whiteprints) and block diagrams, both of which you will explore in Chapter 7. Although you may not see diagrams as often in everyday life as other graphics described in this chapter, they are worth investigating because diagrams make our technological world run.

Before computer circuits or houses are built, detailed diagrams describe what goes where. Diagrams specify what parts are required during assembly. They are used to check the quality and safety of machines and buildings—before they are built. Government agencies examine diagrams to learn if shopping centers or factories meet environmental requirements.

Technicians who repair airplanes or electric generators need diagrams to help them recall how the complex machines operate. The simple diagram in Figure 2-5 shows how to connect cables to a television. Notice that the artist who created the diagram was not concerned with the size of the cables or the cable box, compared to the television. The diagram focuses on how to make the connection work properly.

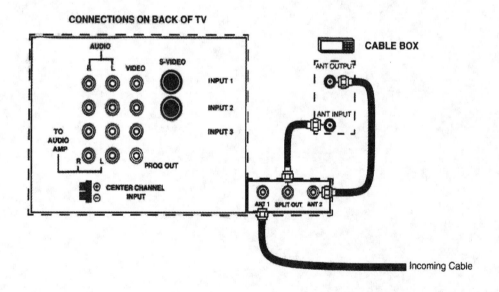

Figure 2-5: A simple diagram

maps

YOU HAVE PROBABLY seen maps in classrooms, automobiles, libraries, and in malls. You may have drawn a map to help a new friend find your house. But you may not realize what a powerful form of visual communication maps are. **Maps** can show you the shortest route across your neighborhood or the contours of the ocean bottom. Like other forms of visual communication, maps perform their magic with few words, relying instead on lines, colors, and symbols.

Basically, there are two categories of maps: *topographical* and *special* (or *special-purpose*). Topographical maps are the most common. Road maps are topographical maps; so are political maps (maps showing the borders of countries, a nation's capitol, or its major cities).

The map shown in Figure 2-6 is a topographical map.

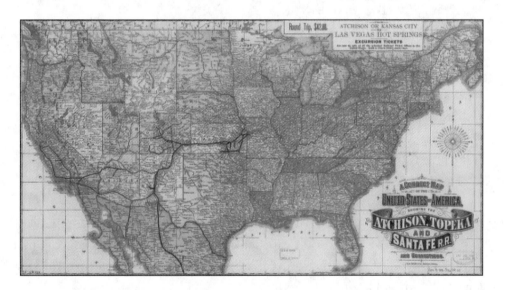

Figure 2-6: Topographical map
Source: Library of Congress, Geography and Map Division

Like all maps, it describes a specific place—in this case the United States of America circa 1888. Topographical maps can contain a great deal of information, including:

- Elevation of hills and mountains
- Distance between two points
- Location, name, and population of large cities
- Location, name, and size of highways, rivers, and parks
- Location, name, and size of counties or states or countries

You probably noticed the word "location" reappearing in this list. This is because maps are most frequently used for finding where things are, including where you are or where you want to go.

There are hundreds of kinds of special maps. These include maps showing:

- Weather conditions
- Population density
- Average income
- Transportation routes
- Areas afflicted with a disease
- Depth of the ocean
- Currents in the oceans
- Approaches to airports
- Types of vegetation
- Recent forest fires
- Mineral deposits
- Positions of stars

Most maps, whether they are topographical or special-purpose, include a symbol to orient you to the four directions: north, south, east, and west. Shown in Figure 2-7, this tool is called a **map rose** or **compass rose**. A map rose reminds you of the direction you are traveling, even if you turn the map sideways or upside down.

Maps are usually designed so that north is at the top of the page or screen.

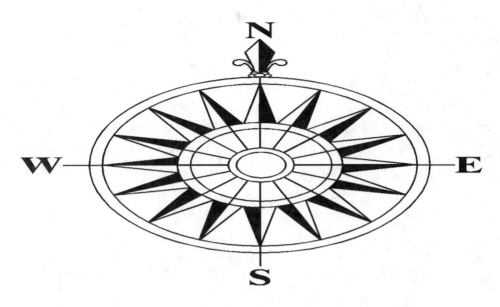

Figure 2-7: A map rose

Like all forms of visual communication, maps may contain more information than is first apparent. Here are three questions that will help you unlock a map's secrets:

- **What is the title of the map?** Reading the map title is a quick way to determine if a map contains the information you need.
- **What does the map show?** For example, the map shown in Figure 2-6 on page 23 would be useless if you wanted to know the elevation of the Rocky Mountains or the capitol of Alabama.
- **What is the scale of the map?** Each map is drawn to a particular ratio of map distance to actual distance. For example, hikers often use maps drawn to a scale of 1:24,000 inches. This means that one inch on their map equals 24,000 inches (2,000 feet) of actual distance.

You will learn a great deal more about maps in Chapter 3.

tables

TABLES ARE THE most common visual communication tools used in business. As shown in Figures 2-8 and 2-9, tables organize information in columns and rows. Labels in the first column describe the information contained in the rows to the right of the first column. Labels in the first row describe the information in the columns below. In Figure 2-9, for example, the numbers in the top row label the innings of a baseball game. The final three labels (R, H, E) tell the baseball fan that the last three columns contain the runs, hits, and errors for the game. The row labels in the first column (New York and Boston) name the teams playing. The columns labeled 1 through 9 display runs scored by each team in each of nine innings.

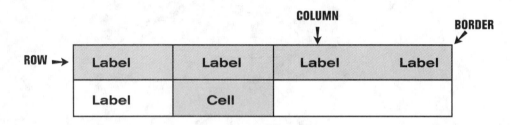

Figure 2-8: Elements of a table

Cells are created when tables and rows meet. For example, if a fan wants to know how many runs Boston scored in the seventh inning, he or she looks where the column labeled 7 (seventh inning) meets the row showing Boston's statistics (two runs). Notice that columns and rows are really groups of cells. Cells hold the table's data, and labels only help define the data.

Spreadsheets are constructed like tables—using columns, rows, and cells. Even the most complex spreadsheets are really only tables.

Tables need not be complex or large to be effective, but they do need to be clear, concise, and easy to use. The table in Figure 2-9, representing a baseball scoreboard, simply summarizes an entire sporting event. It tells us exactly how many runs Boston scored in the fourth inning (4) and how many errors New York made in the game (1). In tribute to its clearness and ease of use, this method of displaying baseball statistics has survived 100 years!

	1	2	3	4	5	6	7	8	9	R	H	E
New York	0	2	0	1	0	1	0	0	0	4	11	1
Boston	0	0	0	4	0	1	2	0	X	6	9	0

Figure 2-9: Simple table hits a home run

charts

AN OLD BUSINESS saying states that a problem cannot be solved if it cannot be measured. **Charts** (also called **graphs**) are great tools for measuring and communicating problems and successes. As with special maps, charts come in all sizes, forms, and purposes. Most charts, however, share many of the same elements:

- Chart title
- An X and a Y axis
- Axis labels
- Data markers
- Data labels
- Legends
- Notes

Figure 2-10 displays a model line chart, a chart frequently used in business. A **line chart** usually presents a trend in data over a period of time. The line chart in Figure 2-10 shows that market share continues to rise, while profit has leveled off. Notice that the model line chart features a number of tools to help the audience understand the chart: A legend (to define the two lines showing data), axis labels, and a data label.

A *legend* may appear at the top, bottom, or side of a chart. Sometimes a legend is placed within the chart (as in Figure 2-10) to save space.

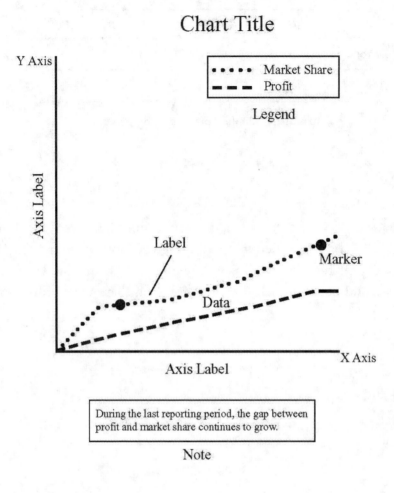

Figure 2-10: Elements of a chart

As with maps and tables, effective charts summarize and translate information into an easy-to-understand graphic. The most beautiful chart fails if its audience cannot quickly understand it. Consequently, the goal of an effective chart is not to present piles of data. Its goal is to explain a problem, situation, or opportunity so that viewers can draw a conclusion, find a solution, or develop a plan. An effective chart finds relationships that were hidden behind the raw numbers or pages of text on which the chart was based.

Creating a powerful chart rewards not only its audience, but also its creator. Very often the person creating the chart discovers a problem or solution she or he did not see before. In fact, some business communication experts believe the most important benefit of business charts is not their presentation to an audience but the process of summarizing information while creating the chart.

pie charts

PIE CHARTS LOOK NOTHING like line charts; pie charts even lack an X or a Y axis. Then why are pie charts widely used in presentations, computer applications, business publications, and marketing campaigns? One reason is that a pie chart's familiar shape gives it a built-in advantage when communicating its message. After all, who hasn't taken a slice from a pizza or cut a pie into slices?

Pie charts have several other advantages. A pie chart:

- Can be read clockwise or counterclockwise
- Lends itself to color
- Usually totals 100%
- Rarely shows negative numbers
- Can be 3-D or exploded, making it still more dramatic

These qualities make pie charts easy to grasp.

Pie charts are useful when comparing the size of pieces to each other and to the whole. In Figure 2-11, for example, a pie chart illustrates the items making up the whole amount of bakery goods sold by Grainville Baking Company. Notice that the pie chart in Figure 2-11 shares elements with the line chart in Figure 2-10: chart title, labels, and a legend.

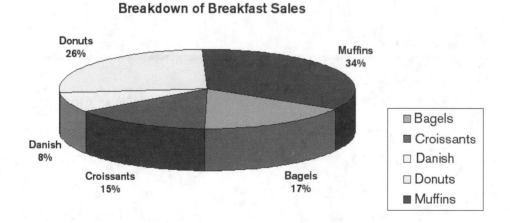

Figure 2-11: A piece of the pie

timelines

TIMELINES ARE SOMETIMES called **timeline charts**. A timeline is a one-axis chart (the X axis) that organizes events or activities in the order they occurred or are planned to occur. Timelines (shown in Figure 2-12) sometimes contain future and past dates and often display a marker to show the current month or day. Besides appearing in magazines and newspapers, timelines often appear in business to plan a project or to report on its progress.

Brewer Street Tunnel Schedule

11/01/00
Coring Samples
Taken

12/03/00
Contracts Signed

3/01/01
Tunneling Begins

5/18 /01
Tunneling Complete

8/01/01
HVAC Complete

Today

12/28/01
Ribbon Cutting

11/5 /01
Track Complete

12/1   1/1   2/1   3/1   4/1   5/1   6/1   7/1   8/1   9/1   10/1   11/1   12/1

Nov 1, 2000

Jan 1, 2002

1/6 /01
Environmental Report Complete

2/1/01
Buildings Demolished

6/17 /01
Electrical Systems Installed

9/5 /01
Computer Systems Installed

12/1 /01
Final Inspecction

Figure 2-12: Timelines track time and events

gLOSSARY

cell—the intersection of a row and column; cells hold a table's data

chart—a graphic that uses symbols to draw relationships among groups of data

column—a vertical group of cells

control—a switch, dial, wheel, button, knob, toggle, rod, or key that adjusts a machine diagram—a sketch or plan that describes how something works, should be constructed, assembled, or repaired

gauge—a device that displays the condition of something, a usually machine

legend—a key that explains symbols

line chart—a graph that uses lines to show relationships among groups of data over time

map—a representation of a place; there are hundreds of kinds of maps

map rose—a symbol that marks the map's relation to the four directions: north, south, east, and west

pie chart—a pie-shaped graph that uses wedges to compare parts of a whole to each other and to the whole

row—a horizontal group of cells

scale—a ratio between the distance on a map and the actual distance; a world map might have a scale of 1:63,360,000 inches (one map inch equals 63,360,000 real inches or 1,000 miles)

signage—signs that explain, direct, and inform; sometimes refers to a set of signs

spreadsheet—a computer application that organizes data into columns and rows; a spreadsheet has the ability to tabulate and graph data

table—a graphic that organizes information in a column-and-row format; tables often have borders and labels

tick marks—small lines that divide a measurement

timeline—a single-axis chart that arranges events in the order they should or did occur

Deciphering Maps and Charts

Ask yourself these questions:

1. **What information do you want from this map?** Do you have a mental list of the questions you need answered?
2. **What is the title of the map?** Does the title disclose the topic of the map, the area presented, and—if necessary—the time period shown (A Population Distribution Map of France in the Year 2000)?
3. **Does the scale of the map fit your needs?** Does the map show the entire state when you only want information on a single county?
4. **What type of map is it?** Is it topographical or special? Does it show cities or oceans?
5. **What is the title of the chart?** Does the title mention units (pounds, dollars)? Does it mention a period of time (years, months, 1990–2000)?
6. **Does the chart have axis labels?** If so, what are they telling you about the data (tons of cheese, barrels of oil)?
7. **Does the chart have markers?** How often do they appear (every month, every quarter)?
8. **Does the chart have a legend?** If so, what is it telling you about the data?
9. **Does the chart have a note?** What does the note add to the meaning of the chart?
10. **Do you understand the chart's message?** Could you describe it to someone who hasn't seen the chart?

If you create charts or maps—or plan on creating them in the future—the Deciphering Maps and Charts list above provides you with a recipe for an effective map or chart. For example, if a chart lacks a title or axis labels or legend or note to help its audience understand its information, can it be an effective chart?

In the next chapter you will further explore the power of maps.

▶▶▶ learning on your own

1. Go to your home entertainment center (video cassette recorder/television/stereo/cable box) or washing machine and note all the controls, symbols, and gauges. Are there any diagrams on the machine? Could a non-English speaking person operate these machines?

2. Why do you think text should accompany some graphics to make them effective?

3. Check out each of the charts and tables in a large-circulation newspaper or news magazine. Which charts and tables appeal to you? Why?

three

Finding Your Way in the World: Compasses and Maps

the maps Portuguese captains used to navigate the Pacific were state secrets. Entire campaigns during the United States' Civil War succeeded or failed depending on the quality of an army's maps. Maps, or the lack of maps, have changed history. Maps continue to reward their users. The more you use maps and the more you ask of them, the more maps reward you.

As with most effective visual communication, there is more to reading and creating maps than first meets the eye. Because maps have been treasured for thousands of years and because maps are universally used throughout the world, the techniques to create and describe maps are sophisticated and proven. So, effective maps are good models of successful visual communication.

Many careers rely on a thorough understanding of maps:

- Earth sciences
- Emergency services
- Equipment repair
- Government service
- Marketing and sales
- Onsite technical support
- Real estate sales
- Weather reporting

compass

TO BEGIN WITH, understanding a compass will help you better understand maps. It is no coincidence that the face of a compass resembles a map rose.

A **compass** is an instrument that shows direction. A compass is a simple tool; yet its invention was a major technological breakthrough. The first compass salespeople must have had a difficult time convincing buyers that this miracle invention really did always point north! Figure 3-1 shows a basic compass.

Attracted by the earth's magnetism—the earth itself is a giant magnet—a compass' metal needle always points north. Knowing this, a traveler can determine

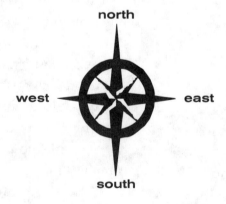

Figure 3-1: A basic compass

the direction she or he is traveling. For instance, if the needle of a compass lies over the letter N (representing north), a hiker who faces in the same direction as the needle faces north. If the hiker turns so that his left side points north, the hiker faces east. If he turns so that his back points north, he faces south. Therefore, if the hiker frequently takes his bearing—for example, rechecking that north is still where he thought it was—he can be confident that he is traveling in the right direction.

Compasses not only indicate north, south, east, and west, they also show combinations of those directions. All directions on a compass, including those between the four major directions, are called **compass points**. Of course, no one always travels precisely north, south, east, or west, but rather, say, north, then southeast, then southwest. All these directions can be tracked on a compass.

Many compasses display more than compass points—they also show degrees. The compass face is divided into 360 tick marks, each tick mark representing one degree. North is 0 degrees (0°), east is 90°, and so on. Air and sea navigation rely heavily on compasses.

magical maps

YOU KNOW YOUR neighborhood so well that you can navigate using the map stored in your memory. In fact, if someone needed directions for finding a building in your neighborhood, it's likely that you could easily draw a simple map to lead her there.

But suppose you find yourself standing in downtown Halifax, Nova Scotia, on the eastern tip of Canada, and you yearn to visit the Bay of Fundy? How do you get there? Now you need a detailed map to answer these essential questions:

- In what direction do you travel from Halifax to reach the Bay of Fundy?
- Can you drive there?
- If so, how long might it take?
- Which highway should you take?

A map can tell you these essential facts, as well as describe the types of land you will be driving through and name the towns you will pass along the way.

finding your way in the world

Depending on the scale of your map, the map might include local historical markers near the highway or other such points of interest and information.

topographical maps

ALSO CALLED **reference maps**, topographical maps are useful for comparing things built by humans (roads, bridges, libraries, golf courses) with the shape and surface of the earth (bays, canyons, hillsides, rivers). Some of the items shown on a topographical map actually exist, such as buildings, and some are imaginary, such as state and county lines.

Maps can describe any place, not just large regions such as states or countries. A directory of a medical building, for example, is a map guiding visitors through only one building. Figure 3-2 shows a simple map, highlighting several blocks in a single neighborhood, drawn to lead a delivery person to 20 West Payne Street. The first thing you might notice is that the map is not drawn to scale: one of the houses on West Payne Street is unlikely to be approximately one-eighth the size of Lake Lincoln. For a simple map, however, correct scale may not matter.

This map has a map rose, so the delivery person knows that she travels south from Lake Lincoln to West Payne Street. As frequently happens in towns and cities, Payne Street is divided into east and west addresses (or north and south addresses) by another street. In this case, that street is North Lake Avenue. (Another way to think of this is that North Lake Avenue is 0 Payne Street at their intersection.)

Notice that left of North Lake Avenue, Payne Street becomes West Payne Street. Its first block is numbered between 1 and 100. Right of North Lake Avenue, Payne Street becomes East Payne Street. Its numbering also ranges from 1 to 100.

Municipalities often number their streets so that one block equals one unit of hundreds. For example, if you work in a shop at 600 West Payne Street, you will have to travel 23 blocks to deliver a package to 2900 West Payne Street.

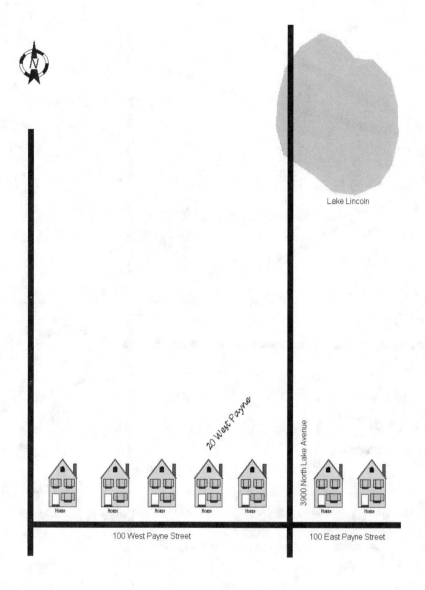

Figure 3-2: A simple map

Although the map in Figure 3-2 is simple to follow, it does not fully describe the Lake Lincoln neighborhood. Frankly, most maps are more challenging to read than the map in Figure 3-2. In part, this is because streets often curve to avoid natural obstacles such as hills, lakes, and valleys; this means they cannot always meet perpendicularly, as Payne Street meets North Lake Avenue. Figure 3-3 shows a more complete (and complex) map of the Lake Lincoln neighborhood.

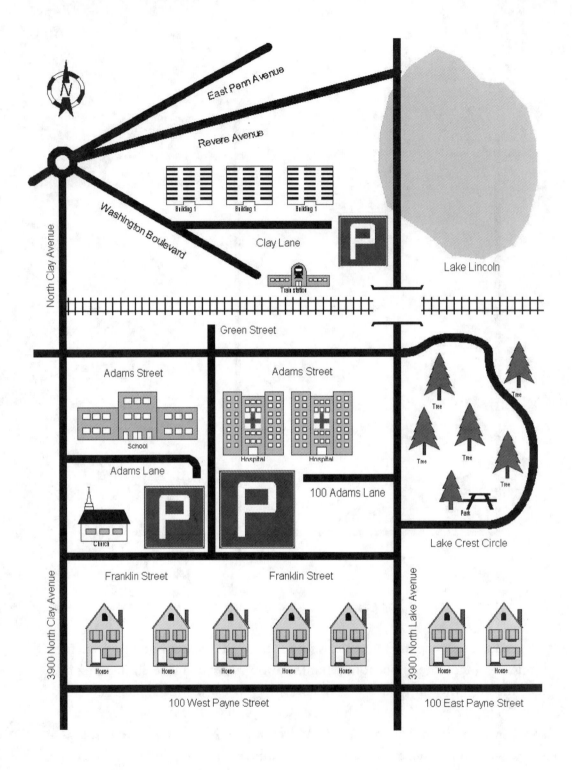

Figure 3-3: A more complete map of the Lake Lincoln neighborhood

Figure 3-3 approximates a **road map**. A road map is a topographical map designed to help drivers traveling through a region. Road maps include bridges, dams, mountains, rivers, and so forth. They excel at describing how to reach a destination using roads and highways.

Have you noticed that the map in Figure 3-3 includes streets winding in several directions? Did you notice the dead-end streets, such as Green Street, or the greater variety of street types? There is Adams *Lane* and Lake Crest *Circle* and Washington *Boulevard*. Generally, streets named *Circle*, *Lane*, or *Place* are shorter, less traveled roads than those named Boulevard, Avenue, or Street.

If you watch for them, clues in the street numbers in Figure 3-3 make navigating the Lake Lincoln neighborhood easier. The block of North Lake Avenue just north of Payne Street is numbered 3900, suggesting there are 38 blocks of North Lake Avenue south of Payne Street to the intersecting street that cuts Lake Avenue into its north and south segments. Did you notice that North Clay Avenue (just above Payne Street) is numbered 3900, just as North Lake Avenue north of Payne Street is numbered 3900. Parallel streets have identical or similar block numbering.

Addresses on one side of a street are odd numbers (3107) and addresses on the other side are even numbers (3108).

Even with all the detail in Figure 3-3, the fact that the map is not drawn to scale becomes a problem. For example, how far is the parking lot at 100 Adams Lane from the hospital? Could a person in a wheelchair comfortably wheel himself that far? How do you pinpoint an address, such as 145 Washington Boulevard?

Fortunately, road maps include a **grid** to help readers pinpoint landmarks. Figure 3-4 is a common road map grid (with some of the Lake Lincoln neighborhood detail removed for clarity). You might recognize the grid as similar to number grids you used in algebra or to the row-and-column format of tables you saw in Chapter 2.

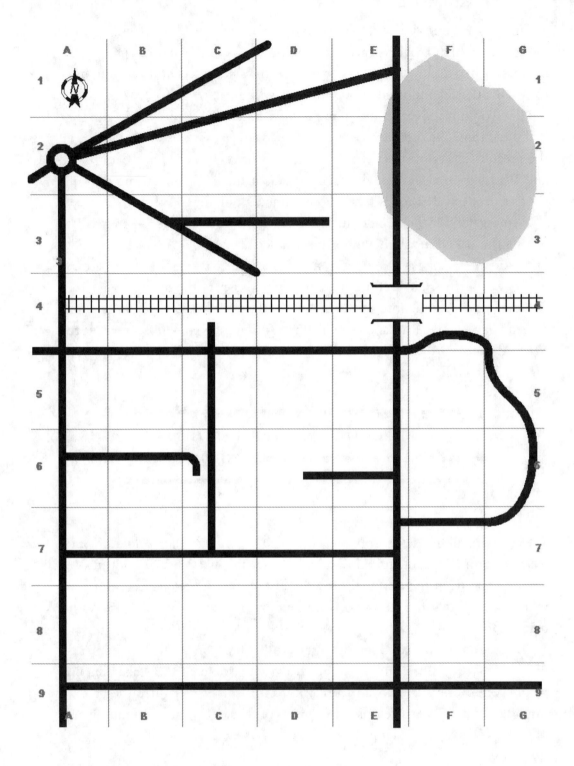

Figure 3-4: A common road map grid

Notice that the numbers on the left (1, 2, 3, . . .) are repeated on the right. Similarly, the letters across the top (A, B, C, . . .) are repeated across the bottom of the map. This makes it easier to track a column or row of the grid. Each square on the grid represents the intersection of a letter and a number. For example, the railroad bridge runs from E4 to F4.

Place the letter coordinate first when describing a square on a map grid: use A1 or D4, rather than 1A or 4D. (The same system is used when describing cells in a table.)

Segregating a section of a map becomes much easier with a map grid. Suppose you are a realtor selling a house. You can tell interested buyers that the house lies within F8 of the Lake Lincoln Neighborhood Map. Figure 3-5 shows a map grid superimposed over the Lake Lincoln Neighborhood.

But what if you are looking for a point of interest outside your neighborhood? You could turn to an **atlas** of street maps (an atlas is a collection of maps) covering an entire county. Now your search grows more complicated, because you might be looking through perhaps 200 maps.

Fortunately, once a map includes a map grid, another tool becomes available: An **index** of the map. A map index alphabetically lists everything that appears on a map, including streets and items of special interest. The following often have their own sections in a map index:

- Airports
- Cemeteries
- Churches and other houses of worship
- Parks
- Police stations
- Post offices
- Schools

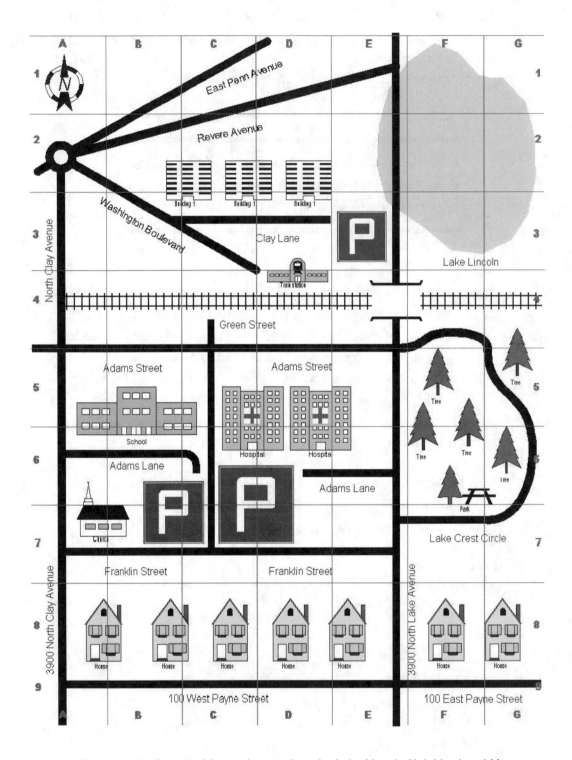

Figure 3-5: A map grid superimposed on the Lake Lincoln Neighborhood Map

Figure 3-6 is an excerpt of an index from a road map atlas.

Block	City	Pg	Grid
Aband Road North 200	Phillips Ranch	14	G9
Abrams Street West 1100	Dumont	23	C4
Abrams Street West 1700	Dumont	23	B4
Abrams Street West 2600	Silver Rock	22	G4

Figure 3-6: A typical map index

You have probably guessed that *Pg* means *page*. Have you guessed why a street's block is displayed so prominently in an index? Cities and towns may have streets that run for miles; you, however, only need the location of a single block. The block numbers serve to narrow your search.

Here are several more tips for reading a map index:

- Some blocks do not appear in the index (for example, Abrams Street West 1300)
- A street may appear on several pages of an atlas (Abrams Street West)
- A street may run through more than one city (Abrams Street West)

Most published maps have a copyright date, the date when the publisher registered the content of the map or atlas with the Library of Congress. A map or atlas copyright date—usually printed on the first or second page of an atlas—tells you when the map's information was last updated. A recent update is particularly important for road maps representing rapidly growing areas. A three-year-old road map cannot include newly built neighborhoods or the highways and streets that service them.

symbols

TO SQUEEZE AS much information as possible onto a page, mapmakers use **symbols** to represent man-made and natural objects. Figure 3-7 lists the symbols used in the Lake Lincoln Neighborhood Map.

SYMBOL	REPRESENTS
	Lake
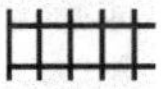	Railroad tracks
	Church
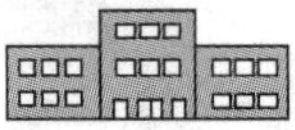	School
	Bridge
	House
	Building
	Street
	Hospital
	Park
	Train station
	Forest
	Parking lot

Figure 3-7: Common map symbols

Although topographical maps share many of the same symbols, the symbols vary slightly from map publisher to map publisher and between topographical and special maps.

special maps

SPECIAL MAPS ARE also called **special interest** maps. There seem to be as many topics for special maps as there are fields of human study. Special maps may illustrate areas of disease, minerals, population, and income. Look at Figure 3-8—there are no symbols for churches, railroad tracks, or mountains. Instead, this map highlights the population of Michigan by county.

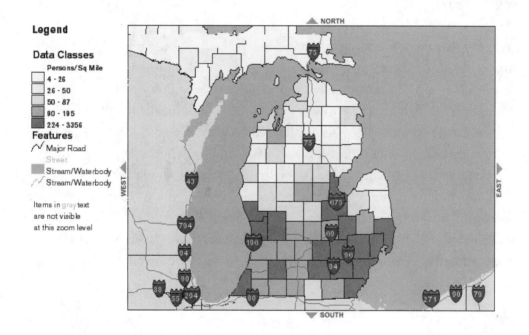

Figure 3-8: A special map
Source: American Fact Finder and the United States Census Bureau

In Chapter 2, you learned that legends explain the symbols used in a chart. Map legends do the same. Effective legends squeeze a wealth of valuable information in a small space. For example, the Michigan map legend explains the following:

- Which shades represent what population in each county
- What measurement the map uses (persons per square mile)
- The meaning of gray areas
- The symbols for bodies of water
- The symbol for major roads

The information captured in the Michigan map could be presented in at least three other ways: As paragraphs of text, as bars in a chart, or as text and numbers in a table. The table version of the Michigan map appears in Figure 4-7 in Chapter 4 on pages 73–74.

relief maps

RELIEF MAPS INCORPORATE features of both topographical and special maps. As do topographical maps, relief maps often represent the capitol and major cities of a region, as well as some highways and borders. But relief maps also display information we might expect to see in a special map: The texture of the earth's surface. They show the depth of the water along a shoreline or the height of a mountain range. Relief maps do this by representing **elevation**, the measurement of land's height above or depth below sea level.

A relief map implies a great deal about an area. Figure 3-9 represents Japan as a country with many mountains and low-lying coastal areas. Perhaps because of its coastlines, fishing is an important industry for the Japanese. Perhaps because of its many mountainous areas, farming must be concentrated away from the mountains or conducted in terraces.

map tools

NOTICE THAT ALTHOUGH the map shown in Figure 3-9 appears to be missing a legend—some maps don't label their legends—a tool at the lower right corner of the map may translate shades to elevations. This tool is an **elevation bar**. For example, the darkest shade may signify an elevation (or depth) of 2,000 meters (6,560 feet) below sea level.

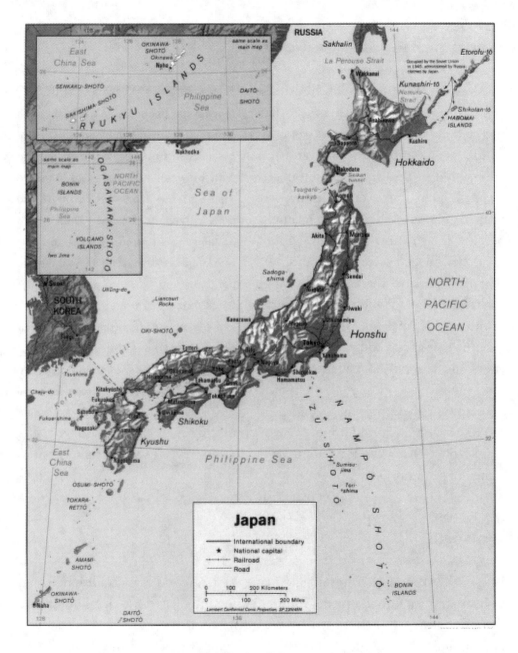

Figure 3-9: A relief map of Japan
Source: Library of Congress, Geography and Map Division

The scale bar translates the distance on a map to the equivalent distance on the earth. Most scale bars measure distances in meters and feet or kilometers and miles, depending on the scale of the map.

place name designations

EVEN THE METHOD published maps apply to names provides more than meets the eye. As you would expect, continents, countries, oceans, and seas are printed in the largest type. Smaller features, such as lakes and counties, are printed in smaller types. For example, because the mammoth Rocky Mountains extend across several states, the type used to label the mountain range dwarfs the label for the state of Oregon or the city of Portland.

Some maps print bodies of water (e.g., rivers and harbors) in italic and sometimes blue type, to distinguish them from the names of land objects. Figure 3-10 lists one way the size and importance of cities and towns can be portrayed on a map. Notice that a careful reading of city names reveals whether a city is the capital of a country, state, or county.

A scale bar becomes easier to use and more exact when combined with a simple piece of string. Lay a string along the path between two places to measure their distance apart—don't worry if the path curves or zigzags. Then, while holding the string to preserve the correct length, lay the string along the scale bar. Now you can read the exact distance, rather than guessing. This technique eliminates guessing because your path twists through or around natural features, such as mountains or rivers.

globes

BECAUSE THE EARTH is round and maps are flat, world maps traditionally fail to accurately capture the earth's features. Sometimes flat world maps distort the size of continents or the distances between countries. For a true visual understanding of relationships between continents and oceans and the ice packs at the poles, for example, globes remain the best answer.

With the immense size of the earth—approximately 24,000 miles in diameter at its widest—mapmakers struggled to divide the planet into manageable pieces. The next sections present the tools they created to do just that.

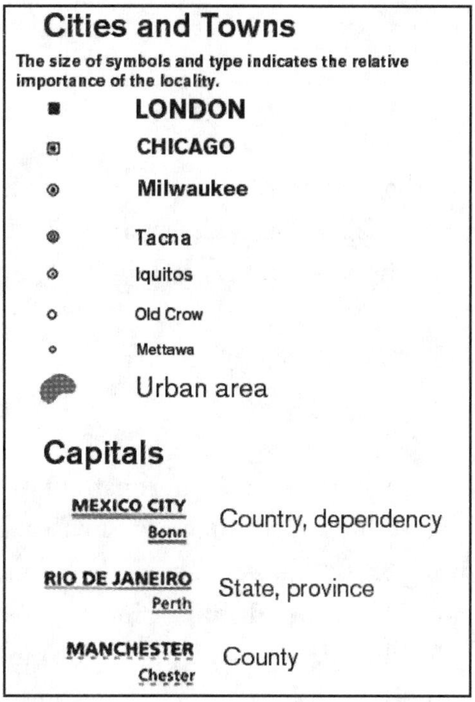

Cities and Towns

The size of symbols and type indicates the relative importance of the locality.

- ■ **LONGON** → **LONDON**
- ▣ **CHICAGO**
- ◉ **Milwaukee**
- ◍ **Tacna**
- ⊙ Iquitos
- ○ Old Crow
- ∘ Mettawa
- 🖤 Urban area

Capitals

MEXICO CITY / Bonn	Country, dependency
RIO DE JANEIRO / Perth	State, province
MANCHESTER / Chester	County

Figure 3-10: Finding clues in place names

latitude

Latitude lines (or **parallels**) are imaginary lines drawn from east to west on the globe. Latitude lines measure the distance between the earth's two poles: the North Pole and the South Pole. Each latitude is parallel to the line above it or the line below it, meaning each line is an equal distance apart. Figure 3-11 shows examples of latitude lines.

equator

One latitude line is key to our understanding of the global grid. Wrapping east to west around the earth's center, this parallel remains the same distance from the south and north poles. It is called the **equator**. You can find the equator on a globe by looking for a latitude line marked with zero degrees (0°). Latitude lines above the equator are *northern latitudes*. Those below are *southern latitudes*. Figure 3-11 also displays the equator, as well as the northern and southern latitudes.

longitude

While latitude lines are drawn from east to west, longitudinal lines are drawn from the North Pole to the South Pole. Rather than being parallel, longitude (or longitudinal) lines curve: They are widest apart at the equator and converge at the poles. Figure 3-11 shows examples of longitude lines.

global grid

Of course, parallels drawn east to west and meridians drawn north to south will eventually intersect on a round object such as the earth. Intersecting parallels and meridians form imaginary "squares" across the surface of the earth. As a group, these squares are named the **global grid**.

Remember the grid superimposed over the Lake Lincoln Neighborhood Map? The global grid performs the identical function on a larger scale, enabling you to locate a spot anywhere on earth—as long as you know its latitude and longitude. Navigation by air and sea relies on the global grid.

If you ask a friend to drop by the supermarket on Hill and Roscoe, you have probably provided the only information she requires to find the store. But how would you help her find the Hawaiian Islands? By telling her to look between 15° and 30° North (latitude) and 150° and 165° West (longitude), you have specified a unique square on the global grid.

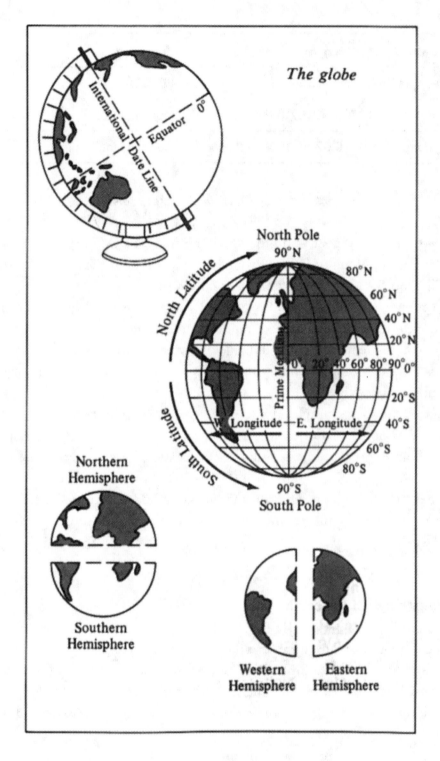

The globe

International Date Line

Equator

0°

North Pole
90°N

North Latitude

South Latitude

80°N
60°N
40°N
20°N

Prime Meridian

0° 20° 40° 60° 80° 90° 0°

20°S

W. Longitude — E. Longitude

40°S

60°S

80°S

90°S
South Pole

Northern
Hemisphere

Southern
Hemisphere

Western
Hemisphere

Eastern
Hemisphere

Figure 3-11: Describing the earth with the global grid

Scale	Written As	Locates
Degrees	21°N, 158°W	Oahu
Minutes	21°18'N, 157°52'W	Honolulu
Seconds	21°19'07"N, 157°55'21"W	Honolulu International Airport

Figure 3-12: Pinpointing with minutes and seconds

If your friend wants to find the Hawaiian island of Oahu, however, citing the latitude and longitude alone is not specific enough. Even a single square on the global grid encompasses a large chunk of the earth.

To more accurately describe places on earth, the global grid squares are sliced into smaller pieces named minutes and seconds. If you divide a square by 60, you create minutes. If you divide one minute by 60, you create seconds. Figure 3-12 demonstrates how to pinpoint a place with minutes and seconds (latitude written first).

Here is another example: If you travel to 34°09'05"N and 118°09'49"W on New Year's Day afternoon, you will be surrounded by college football fans, because those are the coordinates of Pasadena's Rose Bowl. The coordinates 34°09'05"N and 118°09'49"W are read "thirty-four degrees, nine minutes and five seconds north and one-hundred-eighteen degrees, nine minutes and forty-nine seconds west." These coordinates sound pretty official, don't they?

prime meridian

As the longitudinal lines were drawn between the north and south poles, map makers struggled with a problem: There must be a longitudinal line marked 0°, just as there is a latitudinal line (the equator) marked 0°. That longitudinal line would separate east from west and split the earth into eastern and western hemispheres. Where should that line be drawn?

In 1884, an international agreement fixed the longitudinal line to be marked 0°. The meridian running through Greenwich, England (running through the Royal Astronomical Observatory) would be 0° and named the **prime meridian**.

time zones

As the earth spins on its axis, the sun covers half of the globe in sunshine while the side away from the sun waits in darkness. So that adjacent strips of the earth would have the same clock time as the world rotates, the globe is divided into 24 time zones, one zone for each hour of the day as shown in Figure 3-13. For example, if you live in Chicago, Illinois, and your clock reads 1 P.M., your client's clock to the south, in Memphis, Tennessee, reads 1 P.M. So would every other clock in the Central Time Zone. The continental United States (from Maine to California) has four time zones. Alaska and Hawaii stretch into fifth and sixth time zones.

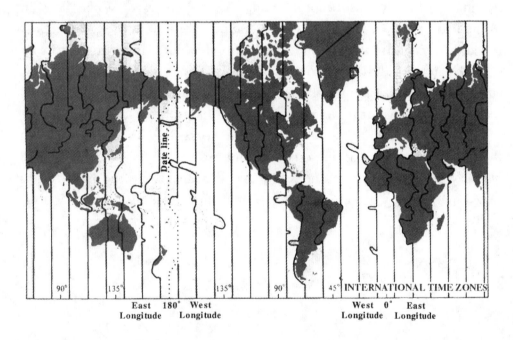

Figure 3-13: International Time Zones and the International Date Line

Figure 3-14 defines how a moment in time would appear on clocks within cities in the four time zones covering the continental United States.

Time Zone	City	Time
Eastern	Boston, Massachusetts	10:07 A.M.
Central	New Orleans, Louisiana	9:07 A.M.
Mountain	Denver, Colorado	8:07 A.M.
Pacific	San Francisco, California	7:07 a.m.

Figure 3-14: What time is it?

the International Date Line

As the earth spins, one time zone after another turns from darkness to sunlight. Eventually Monday must become Tuesday, then Wednesday. Where does this happen? It happens exactly halfway around the world from the prime meridian, along a single, imaginary line drawn from the North Pole through the Pacific Ocean. Called the **International Date Line**, the line really isn't a line at all—at least not a straight line. To avoid separating countries and groups of islands, the International Date Line actually zigzags.

Here is how the International Date Line works. You are a businessperson flying from Seattle, Washington, to Seoul, South Korea. You take off on Monday morning, Seattle time. Once the airplane crosses the International Date Line, Monday becomes Tuesday, even if your watch reads Monday, 2 P.M.

atlas—a collection of maps, usually in book form

compass—a tool that shows direction; a compass's needle always points north

compass point—a direction on a compass, for example, nw (northwest)

copyright date—the date when a work (for example, a map) was published

elevation—a measurement of an object's height above or depth below sea level

elevation bar—a tool that translates the shading of a relief map into elevation

equator—latitude line equal distance from the north and south poles; the equator is 0°

global grid—a pattern composed of imaginary squares laid upon the earth; the global grid is formed by the intersection of latitude and longitude lines

grid—a pattern composed of squares, formed by intersecting lines

index—an alphabetical listing of streets or points of interest on a map; an index occurs at the back of a map or a book of maps

international date line—a zigzagging line drawn from the north pole to the south pole, through the pacific ocean, to separate one day from another

latitude—imaginary and parallel lines that run east and west; also called *parallels*

legend—a key that explains symbols

longitude—imaginary lines that run north and south, from one pole to another; also called *meridians*

prime meridian—meridian (or longitude) running through Greenwich, England; the prime meridian is 0° longitude reference maps—another name for *topographical maps*

relief maps—maps that represent the texture of the earth's surface

road maps—a maps used by travelers

scale bar—a tool that converts the distance on a map to actual distance

special interest—another name for special maps

symbol—an object used to represent something else

time zone—one of 24 divisions of the earth; within a time zone, all clocks
show the same time

What to Avoid

Here is a different approach to understanding maps. These are the things to avoid when creating (or selecting) a map.

Avoid:	For Example:	Or the Reader Might Ask:
1. Creating a nondescriptive title	A Map of Cleveland	What does it tell me about Cleveland?
2. Omitting a legend		Is this a highway or a county border?
3. Making symbols complicated and unlike symbols used in other maps	R	Is that a railroad or a rest stop?
4. Disregarding the value of scale		Is this post office really the size of the football field?
5. Choosing different type sizes when designating similar objects	Chicago NEW YORK	New York isn't the capitol of anything, is it?
6. Crashing labels over land formations	L	Is this an *L* or the side of a mountain?
7. Ignoring colors commonly used to represent the earth's surface		Could this ocean really be yellow?
8. Making your readers struggle without a grid		Isn't North Cedar Avenue supposed to be here somewhere?
9. Saving time by not creating an index		This city has only one school?
10. Forgetting the intent of the map		Why do I need county lines to grasp the habitat of coyotes?

▶▶▶ learning on your own

1. Team up with a partner and sit back to back. Have one of you describe in detail how to travel from where you live to where you buy groceries, while the other draws an accurate map of what you are describing. Make an appropriate scale, such as 1 inch = 1 mile. The person describing the route traveled must be very specific about directions and distances. Compare the finished map with the spoken directions. How could the map be improved?

2. The following questions refer to Figure 3-8. How many Michigan counties have 224–3356 persons per square mile? How does the Michigan map show bodies of water? What kind of businesses or government agencies might use the Michigan population map?

four

Tracking Information

- ▶ **Form**
- ▶ **Checksheet**
- ▶ **Log**
- ▶ **Table**
- ▶ **Spreadsheet**

on July 25, 2000, an Air France Concorde—one of only 12 supersonic passenger airplanes in the world—took off from Paris. The Concordes had an enviable safety record—no Concorde had ever crashed. Yet seconds after takeoff, flames erupted from beneath this Concorde's left wing. Almost immediately, the airplane, the pride of Air France, crashed into a hotel in Gonesse, France. Several people in Gonesse were killed, as was everyone aboard the Concorde: A total of 113 deaths.

Investigators immediately targeted the service records of the downed airplane. Had any critical parts been replaced?

What had been serviced recently? Was there anything to suggest a problem with the left wing? That Concorde's records—including many pieces of visual communication—were about to undergo intense scrutiny under the spotlight of a national inquiry.

So far, you have studied how to absorb and interpret information in the form of maps. This chapter examines the visual communication formats designed to retain and report information: Forms and tables. You will also take a brief look at the structure and power of spreadsheets—a sophisticated form of electronic table prevalent throughout the business world.

As the Information Age matures into the More Information Age, organizations struggle to find a balance between the value of information and the investment (staff time and tools) required to gather and report that information. The subjects of this chapter—forms, tables, and spreadsheets—are ideal visual communication tools for gathering and reporting information.

grainville baking company

YOU WILL NOTICE examples in this chapter from the Grainville Baking Company. These examples form a case study of a business exploiting visual communication to better conduct and—later—grow its business.

The Grainville Baking Company specializes in healthy gourmet baked goods. Through their three locations in Colorado, the company owners, the Molina family, serve an expanding clientele. Along with other examples, the Grainville case study presents the advantages of visual communication in the real world.

forms

FORMS ARE PRINTED documents featuring blank areas to be completed with information. Notice the *printed documents* phrase of that definition. Organizations benefit from distributing printed forms because each user (at least theoretically) enters similar information in the same place on the same document, simplifying the processing and comparison of that information.

Figure 4-1 is a form common to job seekers: an employment application.

Grainville Baking Company

Human Resources Department

Applicant Data Form
(Please Print Clearly)

APPLICANT LAST NAME	FIRST NAME	MI

STREET NUMBER	STREET NAME	AVE, ST, ETC.

APT. NO.	CITY	STATE

9 DIGIT ZIP CODE	SOCIAL SECURITY NUMBER

JOB TITLE	JOB NO.

Voluntary Information

Please provide the following information to assist us in complying with the United States Government Equal Employment Opportunity and Colorado Fair Employment requirements. Data collected will be used only for statistical purposes and to measure the effectiveness of our recruitment efforts. Grainville Baking Company is an Equal Opportunity employer.

HOW DID YOU HEAR ABOUT THIS VACANCY?

O 1. Newspaper (Which one? Please specify.)
_____

O 2. Professional Organization/ Newsletter
O 3. Grainville Baking Company Employee
O 4. Grainville Baking Company Customer
O 5. Our web site
O 6. Career Fair
O 7. Walk - In
O 8. Other _____

ETHNICITY

O 1. Caucasian
O 2. Black (African - American)
O 3. Hispanic (Latino)
O 4. Asian
O 5. American Indian

GENDER
O Male   O Female

AGE 40 OR OLDER
O Yes   O No

Revised: 01-02-02

Figure 4-1: A sample employment form

Although forms are completed with text and numbers, forms are still creatures of visual communication. In fact, the most successful forms are designed as carefully as an effective chart, table, or map—employing colors, shapes, and logical organization to lead a user from the first step to last. The payoff is that well-designed forms save money: Users spend less time completing them (and avoiding completing them) and management spends less time reviewing them. Less time is also spent showing employees how to complete well-designed forms.

Designing a full-page form on a computer quickly evolves into a complex task. You can simplify the design process with a little low-tech planning. Try sketching the form first with pencil and paper. When you have sketched the basic construction, transfer your design to the computer.

creating well-designed forms

ANSWER THESE FOUR questions before you design a form:

- Who do I want to use this form?
- What is the purpose of this form?
- Am I asking for the correct amount of information (enough, but not too much)?
- Where will the form be completed: at an office computer? on a clipboard in the field?

To reduce paper and storage costs, many organizations now generate forms online. Well-designed forms, however, share the same characteristics—whether they exist in digital or paper format. Figure 4-2 offers six guidelines to create effective forms.

Guideline	Comments
State why the information requested is needed.	◆ Users are more likely to complete the form if they understand why the information is required. ◆ Users are more able to offer feedback on the form and the currency of the information gathered.
Ensure that the form is easy to complete	The form should offer: ◆ Obvious places for specific information ◆ Ample space
Edit instructions until they are clear.	◆ Avoid abbreviations in instructions. ◆ Assume the user is seeing this form for the first time.
Use colors and shades to separate sections of the form.	Even if a form will be printed in black and white, use shades of grays to segregate the following areas: ◆ Instructions ◆ Optional areas ◆ Areas completed by someone other than the user
Test the form on your audience.	◆ Ask several potential users (who have had no part in the creation of the form) to complete the form. ◆ Note where their information is at odds with what you expected.
Revisit the form.	After the form has been in service, analyze the results of the form, asking yourself these questions: ◆ Are users confused at certain points of the form (does the form have cross outs or erasures)? ◆ Do you need all the information you initially asked for? ◆ Is the form still needed? ◆ Can the form be combined with another form?

Figure 4-2: Guidelines for creating successful forms

How well did the form shown in Figure 4-1 meet these guidelines?

As the Grainville Baking Company staff has grown, Benjamin Molina, the Executive Baker, has created tools to help staff members track their work and report any opportunities for improving the Grainville Baking Company product. A primary tool is the checksheet.

checksheets

YOU PROBABLY ALREADY use a popular form of **checksheet** (or *checklist*), commonly referred to as a *to do list*. An electronic *personal data assistants* (PDAs) may hold your to do list, or you may maintain your list using paper and pencil. Whatever medium you use, the format of a to do list remains simple: A list of tasks and (usually) a place to mark when they are completed.

Mark Molina, Grainville Baking Company's president, has two rules for his daily to do list:

1. He writes his own list.
2. Items he is unable to complete during one day move to the top of tomorrow's list.

Figure 4-3 contains one of Mark's to do lists.

Mark's To Do List
April 21, 2002

Task	Complete
Resolve contractor's fees	❑
Decide on all hardware and signage	❑
Get schedule for final inspection	❑
Double check flour price increase with distributor	❑
Finalize grand opening plans with marketing consultant	❑
Assign research of location for new store in Colorado Springs	❑
Attend first meeting to select new accounting system software	❑

Figure 4-3: A sample to do list

Resolving contractor's fees dominates this day's to do list, although another day's list will be completely different.

You may recognize Mark's to do list as a basic two-column, eight-row table. Mark uses check boxes in his list. The list brings a powerful organizing tool to each day—a reminder that the simplicity of a checksheet bears no relationship to the importance of the data it tracks.

Of course, checksheets are not limited to small business management. Other checksheets help:

- Students remember what classes must be completed to earn a college degree
- Technicians follow the correct order when disassembling a turbine
- Writers avoid common mistakes when submitting a paper
- Coordinators plan a week-long conference

Figure 4-4 presents the checksheet an Alaskan family keeps to ensure its car is earthquake ready. Thoroughly completing this checksheet might save someone's life.

Item	Complete	Last Date Checked
Gas tank full		Regularly
Car mechanically sound		1/02
First aid kit		2/02
Several days of family medicine in first aid kit		12/01
Fresh water		12/01
Nonperishable food		10/01
Tool kit, including rope and gloves		1/02
Portable flashlight and radio with fresh batteries		10/01
Two clean blankets		11/01

Figure 4-4: An earthquake readiness checksheet

So how do you differentiate a form from a checksheet? Checksheets most often benefit a single individual. Forms are usually designed for multiple users and are usually more formal documents than checksheets, in part because forms are often an organization's way to ensure that some activity or process has been completed correctly or that all required information has been collected. In addition, a checksheet might suggest a series of steps, while a form carries the weight of an organization's policy and must often be approved by several layers of management. Finally, while checksheets are often discarded once they have guided an individual through a process, completed forms are often retained by organizations to prove actions were taken.

As you saw in Figure 4-1, forms may contain brief checksheets within them. The checklists in Figure 4-1 (*How did you hear about this vacancy?* and *Ethnicity*) allow the applicant to check the round circles beside each option or add required information. Circles and checkboxes are used to reduce the time a user spends completing a form or checksheet.

logs

COUNTLESS MACHINES LABOR to support the technologies surrounding us. These machines need to be inspected and maintained regularly, particularly because of their effect on a business' productivity, the quality and safety of its products, and the health of its workers. Logs are frequently the chosen medium for recording the inspection, repair, and servicing of machines.

A **log** is a journal of actions performed at regular internals. A log might record:

- Servicing a truck
- Maintaining a public pool
- Amount and kind of fish caught in a lake
- Length and number of transmissions made by an amateur radio operator

Many logs are subject to audit by government regulators, and, by law, some types of logs must be retained for years after they are completed. How precisely a log complies with city or county regulations can decide whether an organization receives a license or permit renewal, particularly if a renewal is open to public debate. For especially critical logs, regulations prohibit the log from being completed in pencil and prohibit blank pages or lines.

Figure 4-5 contains a sample log used to record the maintenance of the forklift in the Grainville Baking Company's warehouse.

A log might record actions performed during:

- Each shift (as in Figure 4-5)
- Each day
- Each week
- Each month
- Every six months
- Each year

Logs excel at recording consistent information over time, providing organizations a body of knowledge on which to evaluate its procedures. Upon review of two years of maintenance records, Grainville Baking Company might decide to perform engine inspections more often. Or a government agency noticing an increase in burns from battery leakage might require more frequent battery inspections.

Consequently, government agencies enforcing national and local requirements often dictate the content (and sometimes the format) of a log

PRE-SHIFT INSPECTION - DAILY Make__________ Unit No._________

Date	VISUAL CHECKS											OPERATIONAL CHECKS												Inspected By / Enter Employee # / TIME
	Fluid Levels / Oil Radiator Hydraulic	Leaks / Hydraulic Oil / Battery / Fuel	Tires / Condition Pressure	Forks / Top Clip Retaining Pin & Heel	Load Backrest Extension	Hydraulic Hoses / Mast Chains & Stops	Finger Guards / Attached	Safety Warnings / Attached & Legible	Operators Manual / On Truck	Capacity Plate / Attached	Seat Belt / Buckle & Retractor	Acceler-ator Linkage	Parking Brake	Steering	Drive Control / Fwd. & Rev.	Tilt Control / Fwd. & Back	Hoist & Lowering Control	Attach-ment Control	Horn	Lights	Back-up Alarm	Hour Meter	Battery Discharge Gauge	
																								In: Out: / Employee #
																								In: Out: / Employee #
																								In: Out: / Employee #
																								In: Out: / Employee #

✓ Complete or OK A Adjusted NR Needed Repairs (See comments on reverse)

Figure 4-5: A sample maintenance log

Source: Courtesy of Log Books Unlimited, www.logbooks.com, 1-877-LOG-BOOK

The airline industry is only one industry required to maintain detailed records describing the frequency and complexity of service to vehicles transporting the public.

You probably noticed that the log shown in Figure 4-5 is really a complex table. Notice also that this log—as do many logs—tracks the person adding information as well as the information being added. Other logs require the signature of each person entering information. The log in Figure 4-5 succeeds particularly well in showing exactly where information should be entered and in labeling the purpose of the log (*Pre-Shift Inspection—Daily*).

completing a log

When completing a log, hunt for clues hinting at what you are expected to enter. For example, the columns under *Visual Checks* and *Operational Checks* in Figure 4-5 are too narrow to enter even single words. The log must expect the user to insert a symbol or abbreviation to prove that an item has been inspected. Examine Figure 4-5 and you will see a legend at the bottom of the page explaining precisely what symbols are acceptable for entry in the inspection columns. Notice that the spaces following *In:* and *Out:* along the right edge of the log are too brief for long notations. The log must be asking for times such as 8:10 A.M. or 2:35 P.M.

And how does our imaginary dividing line separate forms and checksheets from logs? Logs gather information to be retained and referred to later, perhaps as proof of equipment inspections. Logs often detail a sequence of events—such as a year of elevator maintenance—while forms capture a group of related data—such as an employee's emergency contact information.

tables

EACH MONTH, Benjamin Molina, the Grainville Baking Company's Executive Baker, receives an informal "Headache Report" from each store. The monthly report describes shortcomings in each store's product and the cause of the shortcomings. Here is a sample report from the Denver store.

Monday's 2/4/02 croissant receipts dropped 33 percent because first two batches were singed by morning shift. Conveyor belt broke during night shift, stopping production of whole wheat donuts on Wednesday 2/13/02 and reducing morning receipts 15 percent. Spoilage of sliced almonds from warehouse eliminated almond croissants from Tuesday 2/19/02 night shift production, although making extra chocolate croissants resulted in no lost receipts. Broken water line during Friday 2/15/02 afternoon shift dropped lunch receipts 25 percent. Refrigeration display case stopped working Thursday 2/28/02 morning shift, turning cream pastries into free samples.

Next month, Benjamin e-mailed his three managers a sample table and wrote that he would prefer Headache Reports in that table format. The tabular Headache Report can be seen in Figure 4-6.

Which report would you rather receive each month?

Notice that abbreviations are more common in tables than regular text (*33%* rather than *33 percent*) and that well-written column headings can reduce the number of words needed in the table. For example, by having the *Effect on Receipts* heading, that phrase need not be repeated for each entry in the column (*Effect on Receipts was a drop of 33%*).

March 2002 Headache Report—Denver Store

Date	Day	Shift	Headache	Effect on Receipts
2/4/02	Monday	Morning	Singed croissants	Drop of 33% (croissants)
2/13/02	Wednesday	Night	Broken conveyor belt	Drop of 15%
2/15/02	Friday	Afternoon	Broken water main	Drop of 15%
2/19/02	Tuesday	Night	Spoiled almonds	Receipts normal
2/28/02	Thursday	Morning	Broken refrigeration case	No receipts from cream pastries

Figure 4-6: The Headache Report in tabular form

Avoid using all capital letters (EFFECT ON RECEIPTS) in column and row labels. Not only are all capital letters more difficult to read, but using initial cap formatting (Effect on Receipts) will often save you critically needed table space.

Receiving the Headache Reports in table format better enabled Benjamin to spot patterns in the information. He noticed that repeated mechanical failures were affecting production at the Colorado Springs store. After receiving Mark's agreement, Benjamin began replacing that equipment. So as a piece of visual communication, the Headache Report table (Figure 4-6) illustrates the ultimate goal of visual communication in business: A clear and condensed presentation of information so that an informed business decision can be reached.

Descriptive titles are as important for tables as they are for maps. Particularly in longer documents with many tables, readers skim table titles to see if they need the information within.

As you have seen in this chapter, forms build on the column-and-row format of a table. This isn't surprising, given that there are an unlimited variety of tables. Figure 4-7, for example, is the tabular equivalent to the Michigan population map in Chapter 3. Figure 4-7 contains a great deal of information, but it presents that information well.

2000 Michigan
Total Population 9,938,444

COUNTY		COUNTY	
Alcona County	11,719	Iosco County	27,339
Alger County	9,862	Iron County	13,138
Allegan County	105,665	Isabella County	63,351
Alpena County	31,314	Jackson County	158,422
Antrim County	23,110	Kalamazoo County	238,603
Arenac County	17,269	Kalkaska County	16,571
Baraga County	8,746	Kent County	574,335
Barry County	56,755	Keweenaw County	2,301
Bay County	110,157	Lake County	11,333
Benzie County	15,998	Lapeer County	87,904
Berrien County	162,453	Leelanau County	21,119
Branch County	45,787	Lenawee County	98,890
Calhoun County	137,985	Livingston County	156,951
Cass County	51,104	Luce County	7,024
Charlevoix County	26,090	Mackinac County	11,943
Cheboygan County	26,448	Macomb County	788,149
Chippewa County	38,543	Manistee County	24,527
Clare County	31,252	Marquette County	64,634
Clinton County	64,753	Mason County	28,274
Crawford County	14,273	Mecosta County	40,553
Delta County	38,520	Menominee County	25,326
Dickinson County	27,472	Midland County	82,874
Eaton County	103,655	Missaukee County	14,478
Emmet County	31,437	Monroe County	145,945
Genesee County	436,141	Montcalm County	61,266
Gladwin County	26,023	Montmorency County	10,315
Gogebic County	17,370	Muskegon County	170,200
Grand Traverse County	77,654	Newaygo County	47,874
Gratiot County	42,285	Oakland County	1,194,156
Hillsdale County	46,527	Oceana County	26,873
Houghton County	36,016	Ogemaw County	21,645
Huron County	36,079	Ontonagon County	7,818
Ingham County	279,320	Osceola County	23,197
Ionia County	61,518	Oscoda County	9,418

COUNTY		COUNTY	
Otsego County	23,301	Schoolcraft County	8,903
Ottawa County	238,314	Shiawassee County	71,687
Presque Isle County	14,411	Tuscola County	58,266
Roscommon County	25,469	Van Buren County	76,263
Saginaw County	210,039	Washtenaw County	322,895
St. Clair County	164,235	Wayne County	2,061,162
St. Joseph County	62,422	Wexford County	30,484
Sanilac County	44,547		

Figure 4-7: Population density in Michigan by county
Source: U.S. Census Bureau, Census 2000 Redistricting Data (P.L. 94-171)

Besides displaying data, tables have a crucial role on websites. Websites often use tables to organize text and graphics, even though the table cells are invisible.

A table must present its data more clearly and more quickly than a text description of the same information, or there is no reason to construct the table.

---

spreadsheets

ONE SIGNIFICANT FEATURE driving the sales of early personal computers was their ability to run electronic spreadsheets. By freeing spreadsheets from handwritten ledgers and, more recently, from the accounting department's huge mainframes, the personal computer gave the power of analysis—and the graphical presentation of that analysis—to workers in a variety of organizations and departments.

Accountants and financial officials had created paper spreadsheets for hundreds of years—the term spreadsheet comes from the oversized sheets of paper used. So what features of the electronic spreadsheet caused even the most traditional cost managers to turn their backs on the paper spreadsheet? Here are several:

- Specialized tools allow users to enter numbers faster than if they were typing each number
- Users quickly highlight data with a variety of fonts, sizes, and colors without having to rewrite the data
- Users apply formulas (or functions) to their data
- Users test *what if* scenarios without reentering huge amounts of data
- Users link spreadsheets to other spreadsheets, allowing data to be automatically summarized, even if some data is updated later
- Users create charts based on data already entered in the spreadsheet
- Users lock some spreadsheet functions, so that they can send clients a spreadsheet without allowing the client to view private formulas
- Users build enormous spreadsheets (up to 16 million individual cells, which is nearly the size of a football field)

Further increasing the value of electronic spreadsheets is a user's ability to attach a spreadsheet as an e-mail attachment.

meeting *Microsoft Excel*

CURRENTLY, THE MOST popular spreadsheet application is *Microsoft Excel*. The opening screen of *Excel* is shown in Figure 4-8. (If you use *Excel*, your opening screen may vary somewhat, depending on what version you use and how you have customized the application.) Of course, entire instruction guides—often lengthy books—are written about *Excel*, so this brief description will only attempt to present an overview of a widespread visual communication tool.

Much like an iceberg, *Excel's* power rests beneath the surface. After all, at first glance, *Excel's* opening screen resembles a large, but familiar, table with a number of odd icons. Where is the power here?

You might think of *Excel's* features as grouped in a series of layers, one laid over the other, as shown in Figure 4-9. You

In your hurry to complete and distribute your work, don't forget to use your spreadsheet application's header and footer capability to clearly mark printouts with the spreadsheet's title. And because spreadsheets are frequently revised multiple times, place the date in a header or footer to clearly mark the current version.

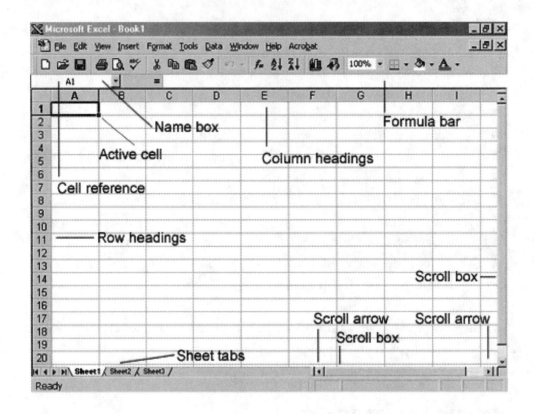

Figure 4-8: *Excel's* opening screen

choose a layer of features only when, and if, you need them. For example, *Excel* offers more than 220 **functions** (or *formulas*), but many users never need more than the four basic functions: addition, subtraction, multiplication, and division. Of course, Figure 4-9 only represents a concept. You can actually format text and numbers and cells at the same time with *Excel*.

Here is a brief list of the key elements in *Excel's* opening screen. Some you will recognize from your knowledge of tables:

■ **Active cell**—the cell currently selected
■ **Cell reference**—the coordinates that describe the cell; if you highlight more than one cell, the cell reference is the first cell selected
■ **Column headings**—these not only label the columns, column headings are tools for widening and narrowing column width

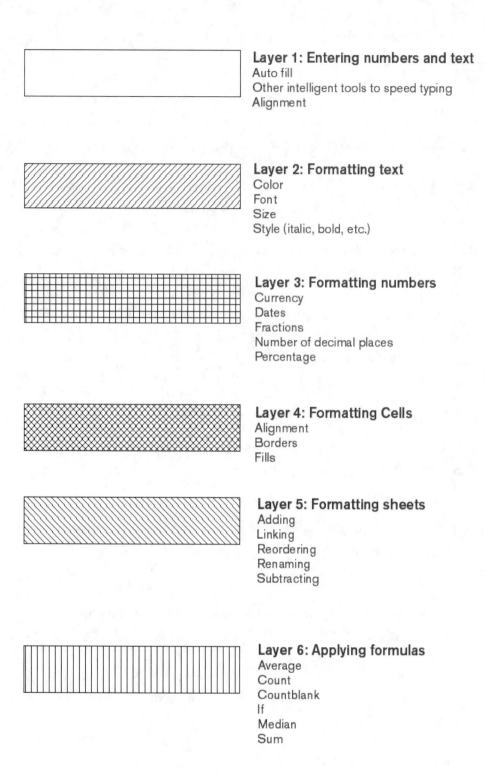

Layer 1: Entering numbers and text
Auto fill
Other intelligent tools to speed typing
Alignment

Layer 2: Formatting text
Color
Font
Size
Style (italic, bold, etc.)

Layer 3: Formatting numbers
Currency
Dates
Fractions
Number of decimal places
Percentage

Layer 4: Formatting Cells
Alignment
Borders
Fills

Layer 5: Formatting sheets
Adding
Linking
Reordering
Renaming
Subtracting

Layer 6: Applying formulas
Average
Count
Countblank
If
Median
Sum

Figure 4-9: One way to think of *Excel*'s features

- **Formula bar**—the space where formulas are entered; notice the equal sign to the left
- **Row headings**—siblings of column headings, these are tools for lengthening or shortening the height of rows
- **Scroll arrow**—moves the display left or right (or up and down, depending on which scroll arrow you use) by small amounts to reveal other areas of the spreadsheet
- **Scroll box**—moves the display left or right (or up and down, depending on which scroll arrow you use) by large amounts to reveal other areas of the spreadsheet
- **Sheet tabs**—moves you from one spreadsheet to another; these tabs can be easily renamed to describe each spreadsheet

A word processing document may have many pages. Equally so, an *Excel* **workbook** may have many spreadsheets. For example, a Grainville Baking Company workbook titled *Grainville Equip 2002.xls* may contain four spreadsheets. They are named:

- Headquarters
- Aspen Store
- Denver Store
- Warehouse

This structure—workbooks holding multiple spreadsheets—makes it easier to track information and reduce the number of files.

Figure 4-10 presents the file used to create the pie chart seen in Figure 2-11. Beside the chart is the raw data on which the chart is based. To create a chart in *Excel*, information must first be entered as a table. Then, using the Chart Wizard, you can build a variety of charts based on that data. Because the Chart Wizard works so quickly, you can try one chart after another to see which type best presents your data. The Chart Wizard even offers variations of chart types: You can create two- or three-dimensional versions of line charts or bar graphs or column graphs.

You might ask if all this variety is necessary. But as you will discover in the next two chapters, not all charts are created equal.

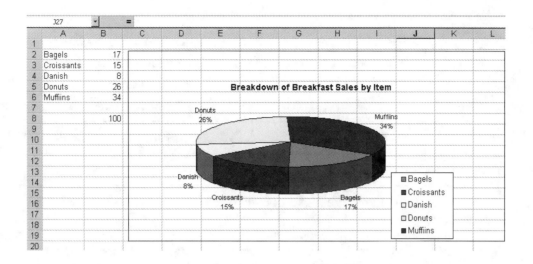

Figure 4-10: A spreadsheet view of Figure 2-11

LOSSARY

checksheet—a type of form often used to help an individual complete a task

form—a printed or electronic document featuring blank areas to be completed with information

log—a journal of actions performed at regular internals

spreadsheet—an electronic table capable of storing great amounts of data, manipulating that data, and creating charts from that data

Choosing Between a Spreadsheet or a Table:
A Comparison of Ten Common Tasks

Task	Tool for the Job	
	Spreadsheet	Table
Create a basic table quickly		✔
Format text to match the rest of a document		✔
Enter great amounts of numerical data	✔	
Send data to client who is not computer savvy		✔
Use data to create a chart	✔	
Calculate totals or percentages	✔	
Hide data or formulas from user	✔	
Use bullets to set off secondary items		✔
Use footnotes to explain items		✔
Sort data by a variety of keys	✔	

▶▶▶ learning on your own

1. Study one or two forms from school or work. Based on your reading of this chapter, how would you improve these forms?
2. List 12 circumstances where you could effectively use or create tables.
3. In a spreadsheet, why might you hide data or formulas from a client?

chapter
five

Explaining Data

letty Schiff, Grainville Baking Company's chief financial officer, has a gift for scouring a mountain of data and finding a gem: A fact or number or trend that clarifies and illuminates the many decisions Grainville's management must make. Given the increasing speed of business, less and less time can be spent gathering information before those decisions must be made. In fact, Grainville Baking Company is actually too small a company for a chief financial officer. Mark Molina rewarded Letty with that title after her charts revolutionized the way the company reports its status. This chapter uses many of Letty's charts as we explore how charts explain data. Although this chapter focuses on creating charts, understanding chart construction will help you become a better consumer of charts.

keeping charts in perspective

As you work through this chapter, you might feel you will be spending your entire workday creating charts. You won't! Keep these three realities in mind:

1. Businesses are concerned with the same issues and relationships each year:
   - What are our profits?
   - Where are the possibilities for growth?
   - Are we containing our costs?
   - What do our customers (or clients) think of our services?
   - Are we increasing the quality of our products (or services)?
   - Is the current economic environment good or bad for our company?
   - What are the prospects for the company during the next several years?
2. Although intelligent management always searches for new ways to examine data—resulting in the creation of a variety of charts—many of the same chart types will be continually reused. Your growing ability to discover important facts buried within piles of data will remain valuable.
3. As you devote more time to studying charts, they become easier to absorb and critique. And the more charts you create, the easier creating charts will be.

before you chart

Precharting Questions
Even for skilled chart creators, completing an effective chart (sometimes referred to as *plotting data*) means some investment of time. To ensure your investment pays off, review the questions in Figure 5-1 before you begin charting.

Questions	Reminders
What scale should I use for my chart? Will I be charting thousands of dollars or billions of dollars?	Take care not to compare millions to billions or thousands to millions.
How precise need my numbers be? Will the chart be more effective using $4.23 million or rounding to $4 million?	If you are charting hundreds of millions of dollars, rounding $4.23 million to $4 million will probably not matter. If you are charting millions of dollars, rounding might distort your comparison.
What interval will I be charting? Will it be days or weeks or years?	Although charts frequently compare last year's status with the current year's status, many organizations chart their progress quarterly (e.g., Spring 2002) or semi-annually (every six months)
What values am I comparing? Is it more crucial to track the number of items returned by customers or the dollar value of the items?	Sometimes you might not have a choice of what to track. Your organization may track some activities in only one value.
What units of measurement will I use? Am I comparing percentages or whole numbers?	Use the value that best captures the issue you want to illuminate.
How will I inject "wow" into my chart? What will engage my audience?	If your organization traditionally uses line charts, try creating a three-dimensional (3-D) line chart. If your company always uses pie charts, try a donut chart.
Generally, what will my chart look like?	Having a basic mental image of your chart helps eliminate errors. With practice, you will be able to scan your data and anticipate the shape of your chart.

Figure 5-1: Questions to weigh before charting

titles matter

LET'S RETURN FOR a moment to the Grainville 3-D pie chart shown in Chapter 4 and in Figure 5-2 below. Figure 5-2 has an accurate title (*Breakdown of Breakfast Sales*), but does that title capture the chart's message?

Letty created the chart at Mark's request. He was considering whether to limit the company's breakfast menu and wanted to know what products sold most often. When Letty handed Mark the chart, he read the title and dropped the chart on his review pile.

Letty retitled the chart, as shown in Figure 5-3, and handed it to Mark again. This time Mark realized why he had asked for the chart and its importance.

A chart's title offers you an opportunity to show why the chart deserves attention. A title should explain your point—the conclusion of your interpretation of data—even before your audience begins absorbing the chart. Titles matter.

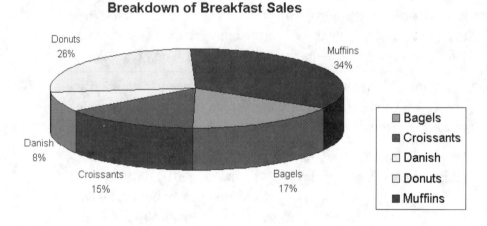

Figure 5-2: An accurate but unfocused title

Danish Contributes the Smallest Amount to Sales

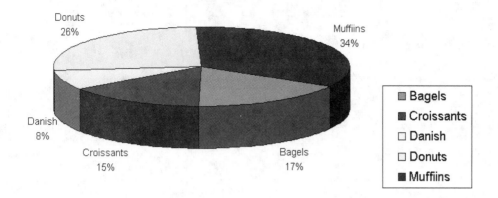

Figure 5-3: The renamed chart

A chart's *note* or *caption* offers an opportunity to stress your most important point.

---

pie charts revisited

YOU MIGHT RECALL from Chapter 2 that pie charts excel at comparing the size of pieces to each other and to the whole. A pie chart can also compare one pie to another, as shown in Figure 5-4, where each pie chart represents a different Grainville Baking Company store.

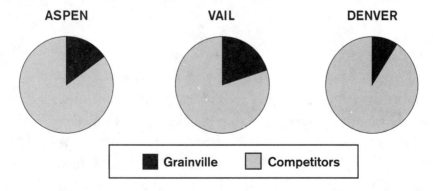

Figure 5-4: Multiple pie charts comparing like data

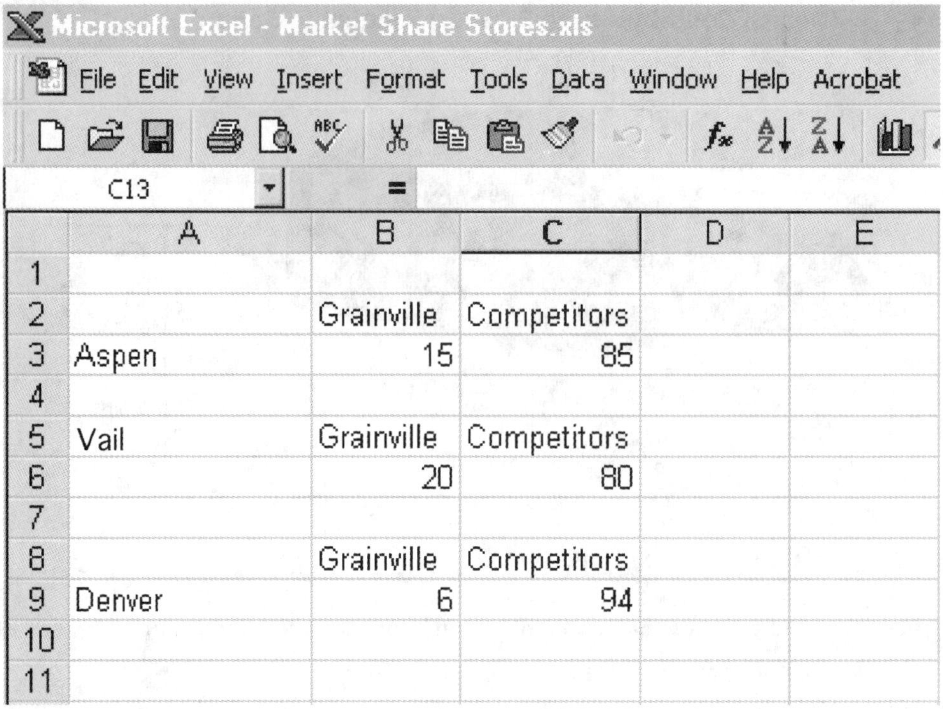
Microsoft Excel - Market Share Stores.xls

File Edit View Insert Format Tools Data Window Help Acrobat

C13 =

	A	B	C	D	E
1					
2		Grainville	Competitors		
3	Aspen	15	85		
4					
5	Vail	Grainville	Competitors		
6		20	80		
7					
8		Grainville	Competitors		
9	Denver	6	94		
10					
11					

Figure 5-5: Data basis for multiple pie charts in Figure 5-4

Here the simplicity and familiarity of a pie chart pays dividends. Do you grasp that the charts compare the same data and highlight the same value: Grainville's market share? To aid comprehension, the fill color and pattern are the same for each chart. **Fill** describes the color used to fill in the area of the chart. **Pattern** describes a design added to a fill.

Figure 5-5 shows how the data for the three pie charts appear in *Microsoft Excel*. Each chart was created separately and pasted together to create Figure 5-4.

donut charts

DONUT CHARTS ARE pie charts, except that their "hole" offers an area for a label. For example, in Figure 5-4, the pie charts do not include how much the Denver store sold or how much the rest of the market sold. Many times that kind of information isn't key to the chart's message, but sometimes another piece of information seals the reader's understanding. The donut chart can include this information.

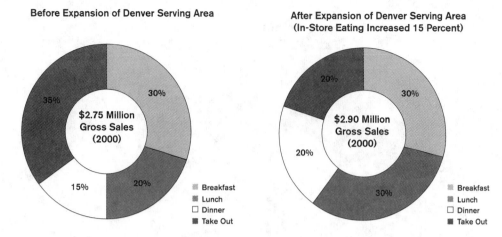

Before Expansion of Denver Serving Area

After Expansion of Denver Serving Area
(In-Store Eating Increased 15 Percent)

Figure 5-6: Donut charts fill the holes

For instance, Figure 5-6 shows two donut charts describing Grainville's gross sales over the last two years. Notice that Letty has marked each wedge with **data labels**, as well as explaining the amount of sales each donut represents.

In this case, Letty used data labels to mark the percent of gross sales each slice represents. Data labels add a specific value to a chart element.

For pie and donut charts, recent versions of *Microsoft Excel* offer the option to label slices with the following information:

- Percent the slice represents (*20%*)
- Value the slice represents (*$580,000*)
- Category of data the slice represents (*Lunch*)
- Category and percent the slice represents (*Lunch 20%*)

Before we leave the popular pie and donut charts, here is a variation of both. An exploded pie or donut chart may simplify your readers' task of absorbing the chart's information. An **exploded pie** or **exploded donut chart** has space inserted between its wedges, as if it had exploded. An exploded chart may be 2-D or 3-D. *Microsoft Excel* allows you to control how far the chart explodes, as well as the position and color of each wedge. Figure 5-7 shows an exploded version of the second chart in Figure 5-6.

Microsoft Excel uses the term plot area to describe the basic area of a chart, without its legend and title. For a donut chart, the plot area includes the donut shape, as well as any data labels. For a line chart, the plot area also includes the X-axis and Y-axis and the area formed by those axes.

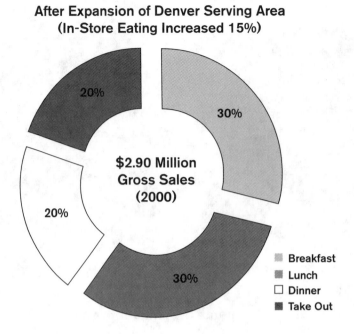

After Expansion of Denver Serving Area
(In-Store Eating Increased 15%)

$2.90 Million
Gross Sales
(2000)

30%
30%
20%
20%

Breakfast
Lunch
Dinner
Take Out

Figure 5-7: An exploded donut chart

bar charts

BUSINESS AUDIENCES ARE familiar with bar charts—not because the bar chart is a familiar symbol from everyday life, as the pie and donut charts are, but because they have seen so many bar charts, in so many varieties, illustrating business data.

This chapter cannot expose you to each variety of bar chart, but the following section offers an introduction to the bar chart family. A **bar chart** uses horizontal bars to track data. The bar chart in Figure 5-8, a 3-D **stacked bar chart**, shows the size of each segment of a whole—much as a pie or donut chart does. Figure 5-8 shows the result of a survey conducted for Grainville Baking Company, part of its process to decide what new products would be successful. The categories (*Milk free, Egg free*) are charted vertically (top to bottom) while the values (*0%, 10%*) are charted horizontally (left to right). Figure 5-8 also shows how the data appears in *Microsoft Excel*. (The dark lines surrounding the data is *Microsoft Excel's* way of indicating which data is being charted.) To make it easier

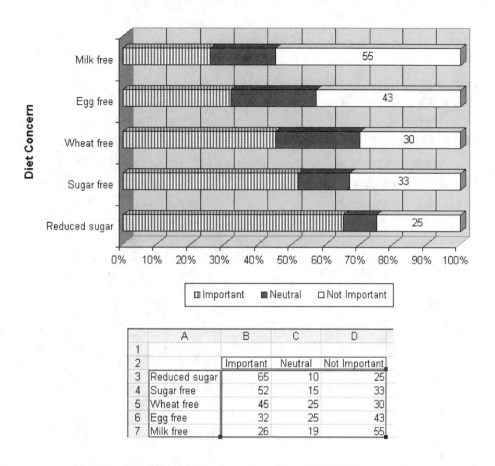

Figure 5-8: A stacked bar chart and its data in *Microsoft Excel*

for readers to compare the data being presented, bar charts—and many other chart types—include gridlines. **Gridlines** begin at the tick marks on an axis and run across the plot area.

Although the pie charts in Figure 5-4 clearly compare pieces to a whole, and compare pieces of one whole with pieces of another whole, the stacked bar chart uses less space for its comparisons. To represent the same data in Figure 5-8 by using pie charts, you would need to create five charts!

To highlight the *Not Important* category, the final segments of the bars are marked with data labels. Any or all of the segments, however, could have been formatted with data labels. The chart might also have been formatted as a 2-D chart.

Business reporting relies a great deal on bar charts. Fortunately, bar charts can be formatted in a great variety of ways to tell a great variety of stories. Figure 5-9 presents snapshots of the bar chart family tree.

Chart	Sample

Deviation (3-D)

Clearly segregates items with negative or positive values, in this case, increases or decreases in cost.

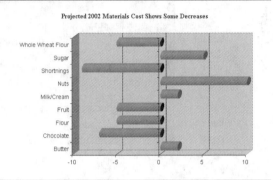

Clustered (2-D)

Groups categories for easy comparison.

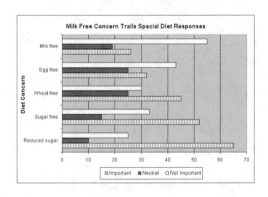

Horizontal

Adept at presenting multiple variances and representing those variances in graphics; also allows room for presentation of actual data

Grainville Baking Company

Fall and Winter Months See Over Budget Trend

	Budget	Actual	Variance %	Below budget		Above budget
January	165	160	-3.0%	▧▧▧	January	
February	190	185	-2.6%	▧▧	February	
March	175	175	0.0%		March	
April	188	192	2.1%		April	▧▧
May	200	205	2.5%		May	▧▧▧
June	175	172	-1.7%	▧▧	June	
July	175	177	1.1%		July	▧
August	180	178	-1.1%	▧	August	
September	205	209	2.0%		September	▧▧
October	210	214	1.9%		October	▧▧
November	300	312	4.0%		November	▧▧▧▧
December	325	330	1.5%		December	▧▧

Figure 5-9: The bar chart family tree

Range (3-D)

As its name implies, this chart elevates a range of values to a single statement; by cutting away extraneous bars (e.g., one representing zero to the bottom of the range and another representing zero to the top of the range), the range itself becomes clearer and more important.

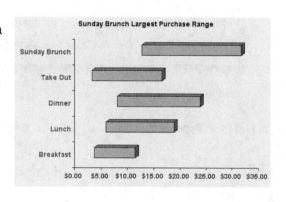

Side-by-Side (3-D)

Another name for a clustered chart; both encourage comparison of values within a category; notice that, unlike the stacked chart, these values do not necessarily equal 100%. (*Microsoft Excel* expands or contracts the X-axis to accommodate the longest bar.)

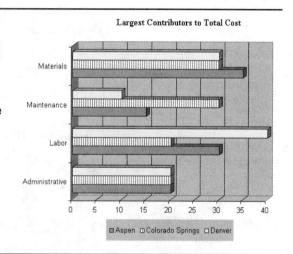

Stacked (3-D)

Defines the pieces that stack to create a whole, the whole—the whole being 100% in each category.

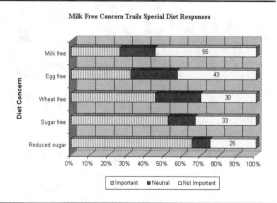

Figure 5-9 (*continued*)

When creating a bar chart, check the distance between the bars. Some authorities recommend having less space between bars than the width of the bars themselves. At any rate, ensure that enough space separates the bars so that readers can distinguish between categories.

column charts

COLUMN CHARTS COME in many of the same varieties as bar charts. A **column chart** (often called a *histogram*) uses columns to represent data. For example, a stacked column chart shows the relationship of pieces to a whole, just as a stacked bar chart does. In a stacked column chart, the categories are arranged horizontally. In a bar chart, categories are stacked vertically (*Milk free, Egg free*, as in Figure 5-8). A range column chart resembles a range bar chart turned 90 degrees. Figure 5-10 presents a stacked column chart, based on the same data used to create the stacked bar chart in Figure 5-8.

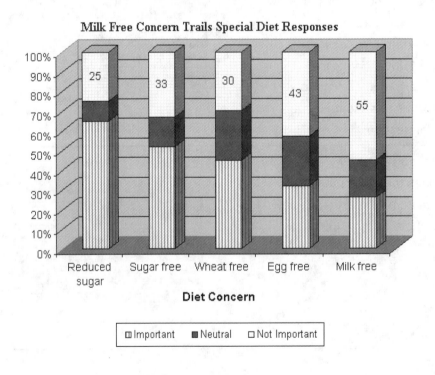

Figure 5-10: A stacked column chart

One key difference separates bar and column charts: While bar graphs are seldom concerned with time, column charts often report how data changes over time. Consequently, you will see column charts in everything from annual reports to computer graphics programs. As an example, Figure 5-11 shows how the average amount each customers spent on dinner at the Grainville Baking Company stores has risen over the past five years.

When creating 3-D charts, double check that your final format does not distort your data. For example, as you change the perspective of bars to add more or less 3-D effect, it is possible to have identical values represented by two bars of *apparently* different lengths.

The chart shown in Figure 5-11 shows that an effective chart can be a simple chart. Because the title tells us the chart will show the "Average Spent on Dinner," no data labels are required to tell us the Y-axis represents dollars. No data labels are required for the X-axis because the numbers there obviously

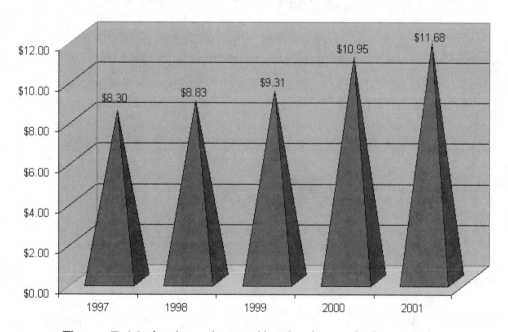

Figure 5-11: A column chart tracking the changes in data over time

represent calendar years, and because only one category is being tracked (the average amount spent on dinner), no legend is required. Without labels and legend, more space can be spared for the basic chart, allowing the columns to be taller, wider, and more eye-catching.

Taller columns or longer bars better display small differences in values. For example, if the columns in Figure 5-11 were half their present height, a reader would find it difficult to discern the difference between $8.30, $8.83, and $9.31.

Pareto charts

A **PARETO CHART**, a special kind of column chart, differs from other column charts in the way it presents the values of categories. For other column charts, any column may represent the largest value, whether that column comes first, third, or fifth. In Pareto charts (named after Italian economist Vilfredo Pareto), the largest value comes first, followed by the second largest, then the third, and so on. Also, a Pareto chart focuses on how often an event occurs.

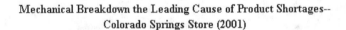

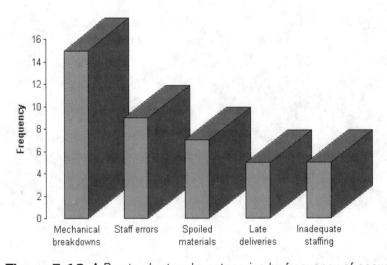

Figure 5-12: A Pareto chart ranks categories by frequency of occurrence

So, what does a Pareto chart look like? Figure 5-12 shows a Pareto chart describing the reasons for product shortages at Grainville's Denver store.

Because Pareto charts rank occurrences by frequency, they highlight which factors or problems should be addressed first. This makes the Pareto particularly valuable for organizations looking to improve product quality or customer service. By comparing Pareto charts—for example, one looking at problems before management takes action and a second looking at problems after management takes action—management can learn whether its actions really reduce the problems it has targeted.

line charts revisited

Showing Trends

You learned in Chapter 2 that line charts usually demonstrate a change in data over a period of time. Line charts work well in presenting **trends** (patterns in data), and trends are a key concern for any organization. Line charts place the interval of time along the X-axis and values along the Y-axis, as shown in Figure 5-13. In Figure 5-13, *years* is the interval shown and *dollars per square foot* is the value.

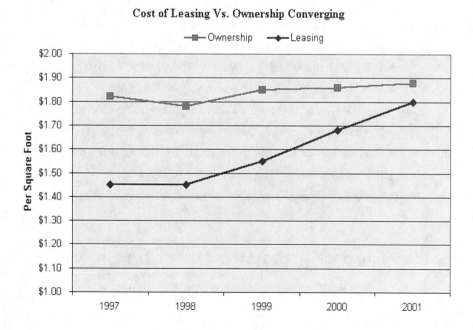

Figure 5-13: Line charts often compare trends

A great strength of line charts is their ability to present more than one trend, as shown in Figure 5-13. A line chart carefully formatted with distinct lines and markers can clearly display three or four trends, allowing your audience to compare various trends. Of course, if you do decide to chart multiple trends on one chart, some theme should unify the trends. For example, the trends might represent:

- Salary changes for four jobs (one line for each job)
- Market share for three products (one line for each product)
- Age of factory equipment (one line for each location or one line for each type of equipment)

Whatever you present with a line chart, remember two restrictions:

1. The interval of time across the X-axis must be consistent. You must choose only one interval, for example, days, weeks, months, or years.
2. The values along the Y-axis must share the same unit of measure, for example, dollars, yen, or euro.

Microsoft Excel offers many tools to refine a chart. For example, three edits reconfigured the chart in Figure 5-13 from the version *Microsoft Excel* initially produced. First, each trend line was thickened, to better differentiate it from the gridlines. Second, the markers were enlarged. Third, the scale of the Y-axis was reduced. Instead of showing a scale of $0.00 to $2.00, the scale was changed to $1.00 to $2.00. This makes it easier for readers to focus on the trends, each of which are plotted within the range of $1.40 to $1.90.

combining line charts with other charts

IN THE ONGOING battle to keep your audience involved and thinking, **combination charts** join more than one chart type to bring a fresh look to information. Figure 5-14 shows a common marriage of column and line charts. Because both column and line charts excel at tracking changes in data over time, the two chart types naturally fit well together. This data also could have been presented as a side-by-side column chart. The combination chart in Figure 5-14, however, uses a line chart to emphasize the trend in escalating amounts spent on dinner. Note that the chart creator could have formatted the lunch data as a line chart just as easily as the dinner data.

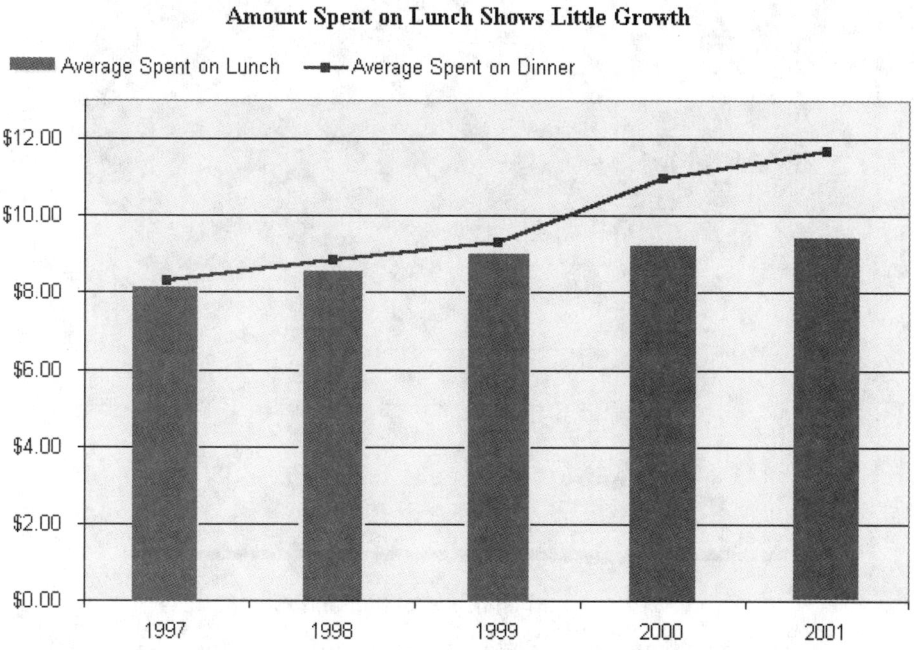

Amount Spent on Lunch Shows Little Growth

Average Spent on Lunch   Average Spent on Dinner

Figure 5-14: A combination column/line chart

area charts

AREA CHARTS RESEMBLE line charts in that they represent changes in data over time. While line charts show trends, however, **area charts** show the size of the trend. Area charts can also emphasize the relationship of one area to the whole, similar to the pie, donut, stacked column, and bar charts.

Figure 5-15 was created based on the same data as Figure 5-13. By making the trends more tangible, the area chart delivers a more forceful impression of the money involved in escalating prices for business space, whether leased or owned. Area charts are less successful, however, in precisely plotting a trend from many specific numbers. For that task, a line chart wears the crown.

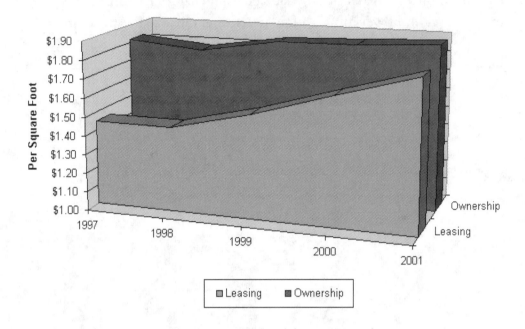

Figure 5-15: A 3-D area chart

Although a well-planned chart simplifies and summarizes, it also anticipates an audience's question. Should the area chart in Figure 5-15 have a note explaining what the costs of leasing or ownership include? If the chart is part of a presentation, would the explanation be better given orally? In either case, avoid sending an audience out of a meeting with an unanswered question. That uncertainty might neutralize the positive effect of your chart.

other common charts

ORGANIZATIONS CAN CHOOSE from hundreds of chart types and their variations. Figure 5-16 shows three common chart types you will likely see in publications and signage, as well as in the business world.

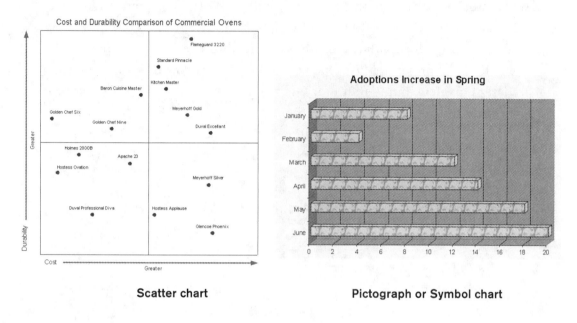

Scatter chart

Pictograph or Symbol chart

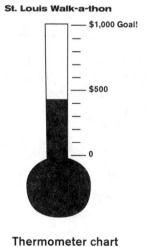

Thermometer chart

Figure 5-16: A scatter, pictograph or symbol, and thermometer chart

flowcharts

Flowcharts plot the steps or events in a process. Whether the process is complex or simple, flowcharts are invaluable for educating people who will contribute to the process or who will be affected by the process. Capturing verbal plans in a flowchart checks that team members understand each step of the process and agree what the end result will be. Distributing a basic flowchart often prompts an organization-wide discussion and involves experts throughout the organization.

Figure 5-17 presents a flowchart of the steps necessary to hire an architect to design the new dining room for Grainville Baking Company's Aspen store.

Seen in the context of building the dining room, the flowchart in Figure 5-17 represents only a piece of a much larger process, but this is preferable to creating an all-encompassing flowchart that overwhelms and silences team

Flow Chart of Hiring an Architect for Aspen Dining Room

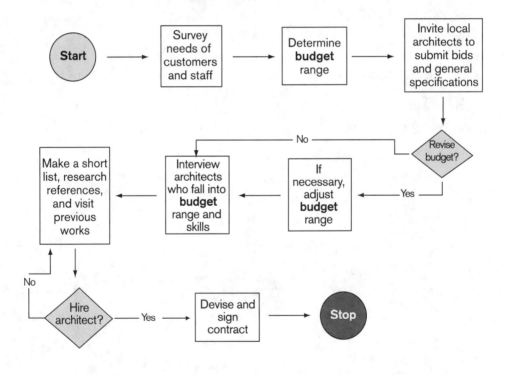

Figure 5-17: A flowchart captures steps or events in a process

members. If a process is especially complex, it should be broken down into easily digestible pieces, but each step of the process must be accurately captured. Here are three important flowchart goals:

1. To encourage discussion
2. To capture a process as it is (not how it should be)
3. To hunt for ways to refine each process

organization charts

ORGANIZATION CHARTS RELY on text, shapes, and arrows—graphic elements you saw in a flowchart—to describe the interrelationships within a group. Organization charts are usually arranged from the top down, with the highest level of management or the most important activity or function at the top. Although organization charts commonly represent the roles of people within a company, organization charts can describe:

- Accounting policies
- Methods for judging investments
- Strategic plans
- Customer service philosophy
- Networking of computers

As flowcharts should reflect how a process actually functions, so organization charts should represent how an organization actually works. Many organization charts include arrows leading from one position or function to another. These arrows indicate the flow of responsibility, workflow, or order of importance. In another similarity with flowcharts, organization charts can grow unwieldy if they contain too much detail. Your readers will better absorb an organization chart if it is broken into pieces, for example, one department per page, than if they are presented with a organization-wide chart with 60 positions. Figure 5-18 contains an organization chart of a realty company.

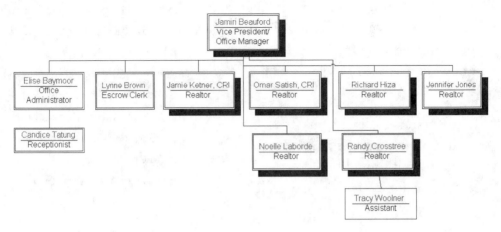

Reality King Atlanta Office

Figure 5-18: An organization chart

If you need to insert an organization chart in a presentation, breaking the chart into smaller charts becomes a necessity. A vast organization chart with tiny boxes and microscopic text conveys little information to your audience.

ethics of charting

CHARTS DELIVER BAD news as well as good news. Even mature organizations hear bad news reluctantly. It is also human nature to want to put the best possible spin on a deteriorating situation. As the person who interprets raw information and selects data for charting, you may be tempted to add a positive interpretation to some troublesome numbers.

Remember that numbers drive the creation of the chart, not the reverse. For example, if a line chart shows a steep drop in profit, it is because the numbers describe that drop. There are at least two dangers to reinterpreting data to create a rosier picture:

- You could easily lose your reputation for objectivity and professionalism
- You could deny your organization a dose of reality

As a creator of charts, your task is not to reassure but to present easily digestible information so your organization can make an informed decision. Consider, also, that it is often bad news that rejuvenates an organization and encourages it to find a new path toward its goals.

GLOSSARY

area chart—a chart presenting the size of a trend and the relationship of one area to the whole

bar chart—a chart using horizontal bars to track data

clustered bar chart—a chart that groups two or more bars for easy comparison

column chart—a chart using columns to represent data

combination chart—a chart mixing more than one chart type

data labels—labels that add actual values to a chart

deviation bar chart—a chart that segregates items into positive and negative values

donut chart—a chart similar to a pie chart, except with a hole at its center

exploded chart—a pie or donut chart with space inserted between its wedges

fill—a color used to fill in the area of a chart

flowchart—a chart plotting steps, events, or activities in a process

gridlines—lines drawn across a plot area to make it easier for readers to compare data

horizontal bar chart—a chart combining multiple horizontal bars and table to demonstrate variances in a number of categories organization chart—a chart that uses text, shapes, and arrows to describe the interrelationships within a group

Pareto chart—a column chart that presents data from the largest value to the smallest

pattern—a design used to fill in the area of a chart; often combined with a fill

plot area—basic area of a chart, including the X and Y axis, as well as the bars, columns, lines, or slices, etc., that represent data

range bar chart—a chart depicting a range in values as free-floating bars

side-by-side bar chart—another name for a clustered chart

stacked bar chart—a chart showing sectioned bars, each section representing part of the whole

trend—a pattern in data

Ten Chart Elements to Check When Proofing

Because charts are mostly graphics and numbers, it is tempting to hurry through your proofing. Beware of this false timesaving. The strengths of a chart (brevity, focus, and clarity) make any mistake that much more jarring. Even more important, you need to ensure that you finally communicate what you set out to communicate. Remember that charts often undergo several revisions, invalidating any earlier proofing.

Element	Consider
1. Axis labels	◆ Are you using your charting application's default font because it's quick to select or because it's clearest to read? ◆ Are the axis labels large enough for your audience?
2. Colors	◆ Is there enough contrast between your colors, so your audience can easily differentiate between lines, rows, columns, and slices?
3. Data	◆ Are lines in line charts unbroken? ◆ Do bars or columns vary in length by the amount you wanted? ◆ Does every category have a bar or column or slice or other graphic to represent it?
4. Fills	◆ Do fills vary so that readers can easily distinguish one bar or column or slice from another? ◆ If the chart will be printed in black and white, will fills be discernable by readers?
5. Legend	◆ Do you need one? ◆ If you do, can the legend's samples be seen as easily as its text?

6. Lines	◆	Are the lines plotting your data thick enough to be seen in a presentation?
	◆	Are the lines thick enough to be seen when your chart is copied?
	◆	If you have more than one line, is each line distinctive in its formatting?
7. Markers	◆	If you use more than one marker format, are the markers different enough?
	◆	Are markers large enough to be discerned from the line joining them?
8. Spacing	◆	Have you devoted enough space to the chart in your report or presentation so that it can really shine?
	◆	Is the amount of text on the page compromising the chart size?
	◆	Can you create more space for the chart by moving a legend or note?
9. Spelling/Numbers	◆	Have you checked even the obvious text, such as your company's name?
	◆	Has someone other than you checked spelling and numbers?
10. Title	◆	Does your title still illuminate your chart?
	◆	Is your title large enough so your audience realizes it is the most important text on the page?

1. You have been given the task of creating a chart to demonstrate the five most common reasons customers receive late orders. What chart type would you use and why would you use that type?

2. A friend explains that there is no difference between a column chart and a bar chart—except that a column chart has vertical bars, and a bar chart has horizontal bars. Is your friend correct? Why or why not?

3. Why might you delete a legend from a chart?

4. You must chart 30 values to create a trend. Would your chart be more accurate as an area chart or a line chart?

5. Why would it be valuable to distribute a flowchart of a process before that process has begun?

chapter
six

Solving Problems
and Tracking Projects

- ▶ **Pyramid chart**
- ▶ **Fishbone diagram**
- ▶ **Decision diagram/**
  decision tree
- ▶ **PERT chart**
- ▶ **Gantt chart**
- ▶ **Project tracking software**

where are we?

CHAPTER 3 offered visual communication tools for finding your way around the world. This chapter has the same goal—making you a better navigator—but over very different terrain.

Chapter 6 features tools that aid your solving problems and tracking projects. By understanding these tools, you will be able to highlight an organization's challenges and possible solutions. In presenting project status, you will be able to help an organization recognize faint danger signs—before they become flashing red lights.

If a vacationer becomes lost during a vacation, she might miss her airline flight home. If a business becomes lost, it can waste money traveling down the wrong path, not quite solving a major problem or not quite completing a crucial project on deadline. An organization that loses sight of its goals and purpose can forfeit a chunk of its funding or can be legislated out of existence.

An organization cannot change until it understands *what* it is. It cannot move forward until it understands *where* it stands.

basic questions

YOU HAVE ALREADY explored many of the charts organizations use to check their own health. This chapter adds to your toolbox by focusing on charts and diagrams that answer the following questions:

- Why do we continue to have this problem?
- What factors contribute to this problem?
- What are the most important factors contributing to this problem?
- How much time will be required to complete this project?
- How much money will be required to complete this project?
- What is the status of the project now?
- What parts of the project are ahead or behind?
- What part of my project do I need to concentrate on today?

pyramid charts

AS A VISUAL COMMUNICATOR, your first task in solving a problem may be defining the problem for your organization's decision makers. The **pyramid chart**, building on the familiar shape of its namesake, ranks a series of values as levels of a pyramid, the largest value appearing as the base of the pyramid. Figure 6-1 summarizes complaints from customers of the Grainville Baking Company's Denver store.

Customer Service Ratings Suffer from Customer Waits

Figure 6-1: A pyramid chart presenting customer complaints

Because the bottom (or widest) slice of a pyramid chart represents the largest value, we know that the most frequent complaint from customers is *Waiting for Service*. The second most frequent complaint is *Waiting to Pay*, and so on, until the reader reaches the least frequent complaint, *Price*.

The pyramid chart lends itself to quick analysis, not presentation of detailed data. For this reason it remains an effective chart format for presentations.

fishbone diagrams

NOW THAT THE pyramid chart has summarized customer complaints, Grainville management decides to address the two largest categories of complaints: *Waiting for Service* and *Waiting to Pay*. Mark Molina, Grainville's president, views customer complaints as a serious company problem, but before he moves to solve the problem, he wants to better understand the factors creating the problem. Without this understanding, Mark cannot be confident that he will eliminate the right factors, and he knows he lacks the money or staff to eliminate all factors. In a meeting with the Denver store's staff, he begins the meeting by presenting the staff with a blank fishbone diagram, shown in Figure 6-2.

A **fishbone diagram**, also called an *Ishikawa diagram*, uses the metaphor of a fish skeleton to pinpoint the key factors contributing to a problem. (Ishikawa diagrams are also used to present what actions must occur to reach a goal.) The "fish head" contains the goal or problem—shown at the right in Figure 6-2— and the diagram elements point toward the head, a visual reminder that the factors lead to the problem. Factors affecting the head are added to the "spine" of the diagram. You will also find fishbone diagrams referred to as *cause-and-effect diagrams*, the cause being the factors and the effect being the problem.

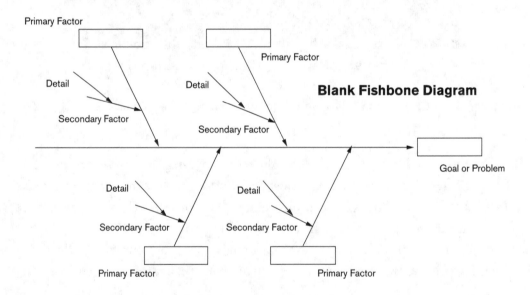

Figure 6-2: A sample fishbone diagram

Theoretically, any number of factors can be plotted with a fishbone diagram, although the need to balance detail with readability often limits a diagram to four or six primary factors. Even a basic fishbone diagram, however, indicates that multiple factors create a problem and that those factors are related.

Real-world factors and details must be captured in the diagram or any solution will be compromised by suspect information. For example, during the meeting with the Denver staff, Mark asked questions and took notes; he offered no opinions of his own. He encouraged the staff to offer frank observations and specific details. Figure 6-3 contains the fishbone diagram the Denver meeting produced.

To build Figure 6-3, Mark used the rectangles shown in Figure 6-2 to divide the fishbone diagram into categories (*System*, *Environment*, *Staff*, and *Equipment*), rather than using the rectangles to indicate major factors. Fishbone diagrams often include such categories, and this inclusion serves two functions:

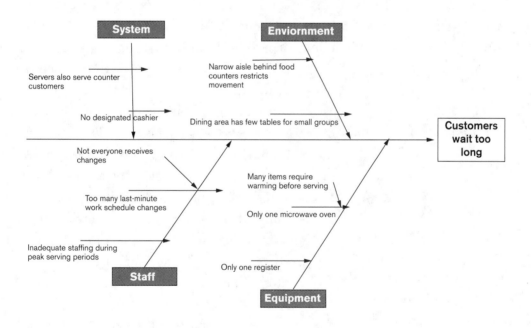

Factors Contributing to Customer Wait Times

Figure 6-3: Completed fishbone diagram

1. During an initial meeting, categories discourage the discussion from centering on only one area.

2. During a later presentation, categories slice the information into smaller chunks so an audience better absorbs the diagram's information.

Quality control groups often use Ishikawa diagrams in their efforts to discover barriers to quality improvement. In fact, Kaoru Ishikawa, the developer of the fishbone chart, was a leader in Japanese quality control.

Now that the factors creating the problem have been charted, Mark needs a visual way to clearly capture the elements of his decision.

decision diagrams

NO ONE CAN look into the future and accurately predict the results of today's decisions. To survive, however, businesses must try. To aid a business as it gazes into the future, a **decision diagram** distills decision-making into a flowchart. This flowchart displays a chain of possible decisions and their possible results. Figure 6-4 shows a type of decision diagram called a **decision tree** (although it looks little like a tree), where choices branch off into *yes* or *no* possibilities.

Someone using the decision tree in Figure 6-4 reads the diagram from left to right (or top to bottom). If the answer to a question is *Yes*, the process continues to another question. If the answer to a questions is *No*, the process ends (*No—next year's budget*) or requires an action (*No—remind Purchasing to complete research*).

The decision tree in Figure 6-4 offers an advantage besides helping someone reach a decision. Being a flowchart, a decision tree highlights any redundancies in a process. As it captures a process visually, a decision tree adds a strong visual argument to a petition to have management streamline a decision process.

Some decision diagrams incorporate the risk involved with each decision and any events on which the decision depends. For example, decision A depends on your company's orange crop surviving winter frost in Florida. How likely is a frost to strike Florida in any given winter? Whether simple or complex, creating a decision diagram removes decision-making from mental calculation and verbal debate and reduces the process to easily understandable graphics. And, once captured in a graphic, a decision diagram can be shown to others for their input and critique.

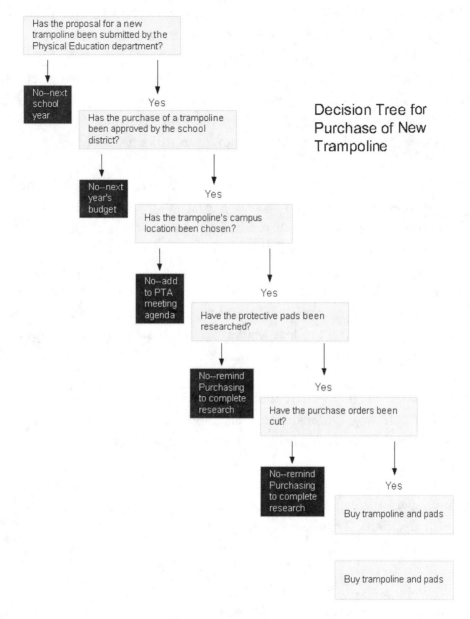

Has the proposal for a new trampoline been submitted by the Physical Education department?

No--next school year

Yes

Has the purchase of a trampoline been approved by the school district?

No--next year's budget

Yes

Has the trampoline's campus location been chosen?

No--add to PTA meeting agenda

Yes

Have the protective pads been researched?

No--remind Purchasing to complete research

Yes

Have the purchase orders been cut?

No--remind Purchasing to complete research

Yes

Buy trampoline and pads

Yes

Buy trampoline and pads

Decision Tree for Purchase of New Trampoline

Figure 6-4: A decision tree

Figure 6–5 contains another form of decision tree. Actually, a better term might be toppled decision tree, because this kind of decision tree diagram is typically drawn horizontally.

This form of decision tree is common constructed from left to right. When it is complete, it is read right to left to weigh the possible options. Let's examine the decision tree in Figure 6–5 as if you were building it, left to right.

In Figure 6-5 the decision (shown by a square at the left) can be made by selecting a situation (*Add staff*). Each of the situations would result in a different financial impact (*Major financial impact*), as indicated by the letter on each line leading from the decision to the situation. The legend at the lower left of the chart explains each letter. By choosing a situation, one of two results would likely occur, depending on whether sales increase or decrease.

Here is how Mark Molina used the diagram to make his decision.

1. Mark reads the possible results. Because the results are in pairs—one if sales increase and one if sales decrease—Mark is, in essence, choosing the best result and the least worst result. Of the pair of results, he preferred results 5 and 6.
2. Reading from right to left, Mark finds the *Add equipment* situation.
3. He follows the line to the left, noting that the Add equipment situation would result in *Moderate financial impact*. He decides he can live with that.
4. Still reading from right to left, Mark reaches the decision box and makes his decision: He will purchase equipment for the Denver store.

Some decision diagrams chart the cost of a decision in currency, often a great deal of currency. Other decision diagrams track less quantitative decisions, for example, which department manager should be promoted to vice president?

Perhaps more than other charts, the decision tree relies heavily on the judgment of the person creating the diagram (usually the person given the task of making the decision). That person must ensure:

■ All alternatives are included in the diagram
■ All situations are included in the diagram
■ Probabilities are as real world as possible

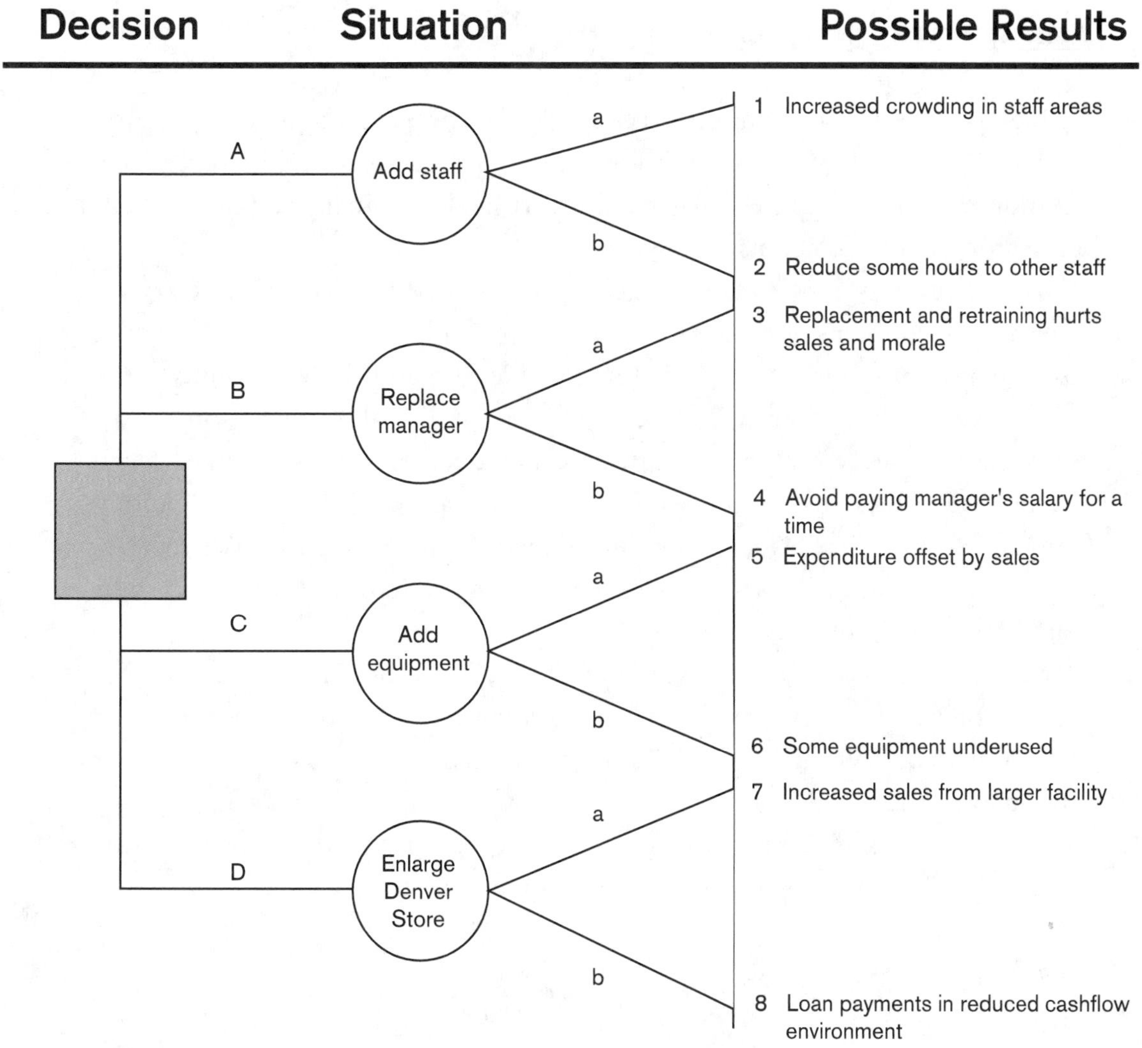

Decision	Situation	Possible Results

A — Add staff
- a → 1 Increased crowding in staff areas
- b → 2 Reduce some hours to other staff

B — Replace manager
- a → 3 Replacement and retraining hurts sales and morale
- b → 4 Avoid paying manager's salary for a time

C — Add equipment
- a → 5 Expenditure offset by sales
- b → 6 Some equipment underused

D — Enlarge Denver Store
- a → 7 Increased sales from larger facility
- b → 8 Loan payments in reduced cashflow environment

A Unclear financial impact
B Little financial impact
C Moderate financial impact
D Major finaceial impact

a Sales increase
b Sales dncrease

Figure 6-5: A decision tree, a type of decision diagram

managing projects visually

MANAGING A PROJECT means balancing **resources**—an organization's assets, usually workers and money—with the tasks required for completion. Too few resources means the project may be late or rushed. Too many resources means the project may exceed its budget.

You will soon discover tools specifically designed to manage projects, but specialized tools are not always required: A calendar can be a powerful tool; so can a simple table. Figure 6-6, for example, presents the work shifts at the Aspen store during Grainville Baking Company's busy holiday season.

Figure 6-6 was created in *Excel* by entering letters and fill colors in each cell to represent the shifts (*B* = breakfast, *L* = lunch, and *D* = dinner). By pasting an *Excel* formula in the far right column, the person creating the table receives updated totals in the far right column, allowing her to monitor that the shifts are fairly distributed.

Just as the person who created the work schedule monitors the total number of shifts for each worker, project managers monitor a variety of dynamic values to do their jobs. With projects including team members across the country—or throughout the world—project managers must deal with different languages, different time zones, and different currency. This complexity has driven project managers away from paper scheduling to electronic tools. For example, if employee

Shift	1	2	3	4	5	6	7	8	9	10	11	12	13	14	Total
Alicia	D	D	D		D	D	D		B	B	B	B		B	11
Bernice	L		L	L	L	L	L		B	B	B		B	B	11
Derek	B	B		B	B	B	B	B		L	L	L			10
Jonathan		L	L		L	L	L	L	L			B	B	L	10
Juan	D	L	L	D	D				D	D	D	D		D	10
Larry	B	D	D	D		B	L	B	B		L	L	L		11
Melonie	B	B	B	B	B			D	D	L			L	L	10
Sanjay	L	L	B	L		L	D	L		L	L	L		L	11
Stanley	D	D	D	D		D	D		L	D	D	D	D		11
Wendy	L	B	L	L	L		B	L		D			D	D	10
Zoe	B	L	B		D	B	B	D	L		B	B	L		11

(Column group header: December, spanning columns 1–14)

Figure 6-6: A table as schedule tool

Jonathan breaks his leg skiing, the work schedule in Figure 6-6 becomes obsolete and must be redone. Certainly, that would take some time. But imagine if a flood delays delivery of steel beams, forcing the rescheduling of a yearlong airport expansion project. Who would want to do that rescheduling on paper?

Fortunately, project managers have access to several tools to help them visualize projects and schedules from the project's early life.

PERT charts

PROGRAM EVALUATION AND REVIEW TECHNIQUE (PERT) charts, introduced in the late 1950s as part of the United States Navy's Polaris program, help managers analyze, monitor, and plan by representing projects with multiple, interdependent tasks. PERT charts place activities and events in a single framework, employing symbols and arrows to illustrate the sequential order of steps needed to complete a project.

Figure 6-7 contains a simplified PERT chart showing three activities and a definition of the information in each box.

Figure 6-7: A sample PERT chart

Frequently used for large projects, PERT charts excel at presenting schedulers with a project overview, particularly highlighting dependent tasks. The PERT chart in Figure 6-7 indicates dependency between tasks by using arrows to show how the *Painting the Denver Store* activity leads to the *Replacing the Denver store signage* activity. **Dependency** refers to a relationship established between two tasks that tie when one task starts or finishes to the other task's status.

The boxes in Figure 6-7 condense crucial project information into an admirably small space. The first box (on the left) contains six pieces of data (excluding the task name). Reading from the upper left, here is what they stand for:

- **Early Start**—the earliest date the task will likely begin
- **Duration**—the estimated amount of time required to complete a task
- **Early Finish**—the earliest date the task will likely finish
- **Late Start**—the latest date a task can begin and not delay the overall project deadline
- **Slack**—describes the time a task can be delayed before it becomes a critical task (also called *float*); box 1 and 2 have slack; box 3 does not
- **Late Finish**—the latest date a task can finish and not delay the overall project deadline

Interpreting this information, we see slack in the schedule of the first two tasks. Task 1 (box 1) can end any time between 11/8/01 and 11/12/01. If Task 1 ends after 11/12/01, however, it affects Task 2. Task 3 has no slack. For whatever reason, Task 3 must be done immediately because Figure 6-5 on page 117 contains a PERT chart of the major Grainville Baking Company project: Enlarging the Denver store.

Many PERT charts include information on each task's duration and the workers assigned to the task. Although they look like diagrams of odd dance steps, PERT charts frequently root out redundant activities or misplaced events.

PERT charts also offer a clear description of a project's critical tasks and critical path. A **critical task** must be completed on time for a project to finish on time. In Figure 6-8, for example, *Receive loan approval from bank* is a critical task. A series of critical tasks form a **critical path**, highlighted in Figure 6-8 with a thick line and arrows. Project managers monitor their critical paths carefully.

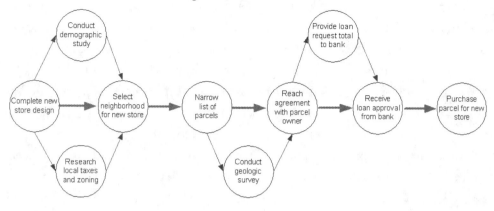

Selecting a Location for New Store

Figure 6-8: A PERT chart displays activities and events in sequential order

No wonder the **Critical Path Method** (CPM) remains a common technique for managing projects. CPM charts are so similar to PERT charts that CPM charts are often titled CPM/PERT charts.

PERT charts are less effective with overlapping tasks. The PERT chart's basic design assumes that one event ends before another begins. Chart creators must clearly define activities and their relation to other activities.

Gantt charts

If your work includes tracking project schedule and cost (both are often referred to as project controls) expect your charts to be revised. Large projects are especially effected by unforeseen events. Store multiple versions of your charts in case you are asked to reproduce earlier plans.

WHEN IT COMES to representing projects and their tasks, the electronic Gantt chart is king. As you will see later, *Microsoft Project*, the most popular project management software, builds Gantt charts to represent projects and their tasks—as do many other specialized project management software. So what is it about Gantt charts that make them valuable among people who make their living managing projects?

Gantt charts, first created by Charles Gantt in 1917, translate a series of start and end dates into horizontal bars representing duration. In essence, each of the horizontal bars is a timeline. Once you see a task's timeline, you can compare that timeline with other task's timelines. Notice that Gantt charts do a good job of visualizing tasks that overlap. The trick for project managers is spotting when tasks conflict and making sure that the right tasks complete first.

You no doubt realized that the longer the task duration, the longer the bar representing it. You may also have noticed that Gantt charts are half spreadsheet (the left columns) and half chart (the horizontal bars).

Although Gantt charts also provide raw data in the *Start*, *End*, and *Duration* columns, those horizontal bars offer the quickest way to compare durations. For example, study Figure 6-9, covering all parts of the chart to the right of the *Duration* column. Can you find those tasks that occur during the time the warehouse will be expanded? Did you have to recalculate—glancing at the warehouse schedule repeatedly? Did you want to peek at the bars? For the record, tasks 2 through 13 are scheduled for completion during the warehouse expansion project.

Electronic Gantt charts are able to report durations in a variety of scales. The time scale in Figure 6-9 displays task durations in weeks. Tasks requiring one day to complete, for instance, *Graphics Contractor Selected*, appear as thin bars. For more refined scrutiny, a project manager could display duration in days,

ID	Task Name	Start	End	Duration
1	Warehouse Expansion	4/2/01	6/15/01	55 d
2	Planning Meeting	4/9/01	4/10/01	2 d
3	Customer Services Offices Built	4/2/01	5/18/01	35 d
4	Market Research	4/12/01	5/9/01	20 d
5	Vendor Research	4/16/01	4/25/01	8 d
6	Graphics Contractor Selected	5/2/01	5/2/01	1 d
7	Final Product Selection	6/4/01	6/5/01	2 d
8	Catalog Design	5/7/01	6/1/01	20 d
9	Product Photography	6/11/01	6/13/01	3 d
10	Catalog Printer Selected	5/10/01	5/10/01	1 d
11	Final Warehouse Inspection	6/11/01	6/11/01	1 d
12	Photography Review	6/14/01	6/14/01	1 d
13	Catalog Design Review	6/5/01	6/8/01	4 d
14	Cust Serv Furnishings Installed	6/15/01	6/22/01	6 d
15	Catalog to Printer	7/2/01	7/2/01	1 d
16	Customer Serv Reps Trained	7/9/01	7/20/01	10 d
17	Catalogs Printed	7/3/01	7/16/01	10 d
18	Catalogs Mailed/Shipped to Stores	7/17/01	7/24/01	6 d

Figure 6-9: A Gantt chart reporting on a four-month project

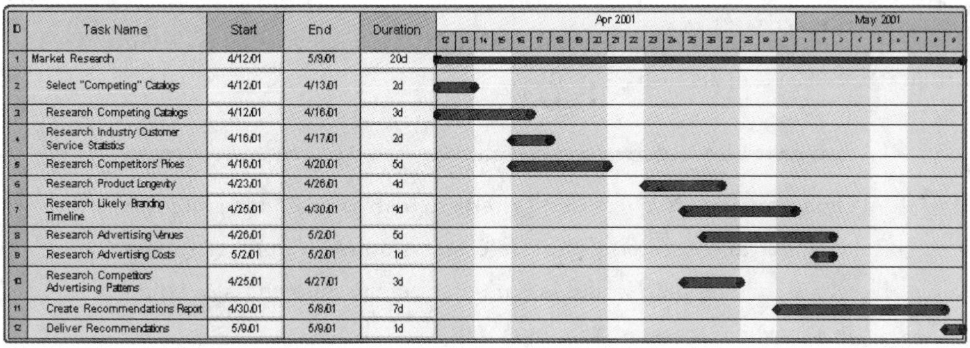

Figure 6-10: A Gantt chart focusing on a single task of Figure 6-9

giving more representation to short-duration tasks but creating a much wider chart (the chart would be wider because seven days would no longer be represented by a single week).

Gantt charts can also drill down (reveal detail) a single task to see its components. For example, Figure 6-10 shows a Gantt chart reporting on the tasks within task 4, *Market Research*.

Compare the appearance of items in this *Task Name* column with the Gantt chart in Figure 6-9. Each task below *Market Research* is indented. Gantt charts commonly use these techniques to show that the indented tasks are part of a larger task—in this case, completing the *Market Research*.

Three other types of task dependencies are possible. Finish-to-start means one task must finish before another task starts. Start-to-finish means a second task can finish only after the first task starts. A start-to-start dependency means two tasks start at the same time.

In the language of project management, the *Market Research* task and the tasks under it have a **finish–to–finish dependency** relationship, meaning that the *Market Research* task cannot be completed until all the tasks under it have been completed.

Two other differences in Figure 6-10 are worth mentioning. First, the timeline representing *Market Research* summarizes all the timelines below it. In other words, the *Market Research* timeline begins when the first task begins and ends when the last task ends. Second, the time scale for this Gantt chart is days rather than weeks, allowing even two-day projects a more noticeable timeline.

Some Gantt charts also include the name of the person responsible for completing a task beside each task, showing project management who to contact if a task falls behind schedule.

Organizations often use Gantt charts to test "what if" scenarios. An engineer might enter a start date and a duration number to see where the end date would fall or enter an end date and a duration to see where the start date must fall.

For all their power to represent complex information vividly, Gantt charts are not perfect. Although they detail the status of a project's tasks, Gantt charts do not indicate whether the entire project has fallen behind schedule, maintained its schedule, or is ahead of schedule.

Project managers loathe surprises. If your charting reveals a problem a project manager should be aware of, notify the project manager immediately. You will give the manager an opportunity to weigh possible actions.

project tracking software

Today *Microsoft Project* rules as the most popular project management software, and in the following brief look at electronic project tracking, *Microsoft Project* serves as our model. Although *Microsoft Project* offers a variety of ways to view your project, we will concentrate on its Gantt charting features. As with ink-and-paper Gantt charts, *Microsoft Project* compares where your project stands with where it should stand. A crucial tool in presenting this sometimes troubling status is the project baseline.

A project's **baseline** grows from the best current information mixed with the best estimate of future conditions. A baseline addresses these basic concerns:

- When do you expect a project to begin?
- When do you expect a project to end?
- How long you expect a project to run?
- How much you expect a project to cost?
- How many workers do you expect the project to require?

Even the most complicated project plan must begin somewhere, even if that somewhere is only an educated estimate. The original project baseline is that estimate. Just as a flowchart often serves as a trial balloon to begin discussion and feedback, distribution of an original baseline serves as a starting point for discussion and feedback. A baseline gives a project manager a crucial measuring stick with which to compare the actual project. Without a baseline, a project manager would not know if the project was ahead or behind expectations.

For complex projects, managers use more than one baseline. Although the entire project has a baseline, each significant segment of the project may have its own baseline. Major public works projects, for example, have books of Gantt charts, and each major task within the project has its own baseline; so do many minor tasks.

Let's begin our exploration of *Microsoft Project* with its opening screen, shown in Figure 6-11.

You probably already noticed the familiar Gantt chart structure in Figure 6-11. The vertical bars in the right section of the Gantt chart shows that *Project* considers Saturday and Sunday nonwork days, although this can be customized. The scroll bars at the bottom of the Gantt chart allow you to scroll through task descriptions or the time line. You can scroll months into the future or past with these scroll bars.

Because of its concern for scheduling, *Project* keeps a calendar nearby. Beside it being one of the views available from the opening screen, many of *Project's* dialog boxes allow you to access a calendar to select dates. Figure 6-12 contains a typical *Project* dialog box, with a calendar available from a drop down list.

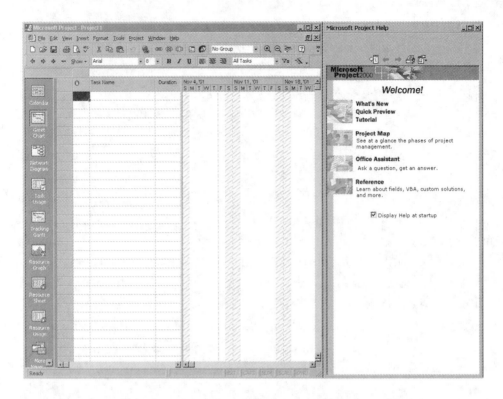

Figure 6-11: *Microsoft Project's* opening window

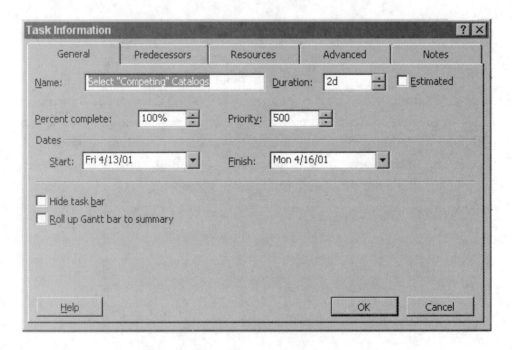

Figure 6-12: A typical *Microsoft Project* dialog box (note the calendar)

Because *Microsoft Project* devotes itself to presenting project management information—unlike *Microsoft Excel*—it offers multiple views of project management status. Figure 6-13 shows one of those views.

First, notice that the tasks charted here are the same tasks shown in Figure 6-10 (although the overall *Market Research* task has been eliminated). Second, notice that the dates for the tasks are changed. More about the changed dates in a moment. Third, notice that there are a great many more dates in Figure 6-13. Fourth, notice that there are more graphics in this Gantt chart than the Gantt chart in Figure 6-10. So, what does this all mean?

The Gantt chart captured in Figure 6-13 shows variance. **Variance** (sometimes called the *delta*) describes the gap between where you should be—based on your project plan—and where you are, based on actual data. Variance comes in two flavors:

1. Good variance means the project stands ahead of its schedule or below its cost.

2. Bad variance means the project stands behind its schedule or over its cost.

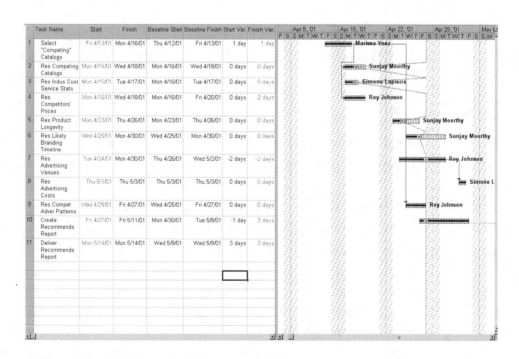

Figure 6-13: A *Microsoft Project* Gantt chart tracking variance from project schedule

The Gantt chart in Figure 6–13 shows variance three ways:

1. The *Start Var.* column shows variance in the start dates: no variance (*0 days*), ahead of schedule (*-2*), or behind schedule (*3 days*).
2. The *Finish Var.* column shows whether there is no variance (*0 days*), ahead of schedule variance (*-2 days*) or behind schedule variance (*3 days*).
3. The progress line, which veers across the horizontal-bar section of the Gantt chart, highlights tasks that are behind schedule.

Before creating a progress line, *Project* needs to know the **status date** on which you want to base your variance chart. The status date could be today's date or any date relevant to the project. Based on the status date—the date chosen was Friday, April 27, 2001—*Project* draws a line from April 27, 2001 to the bottom of the chart, veering to the left to indicate a task behind schedule. This is a **progress line**.

To fill the *Start Var.* and *Finish Var.* columns, *Project* needs two sets of dates: The actual start and finish dates (shown in the *Start* and *Finish* columns) and the baseline start and baseline finish dates (shown in the *Baseline Start* and *Baseline Finish* columns).

The difference between Figure 6–10's and Figure 6–13's start and finish dates reflects the actual data reported in Figure 6–13. For example, the first task (*Select "Competing" Catalogs*) did not begin on April 12, 2001, as it was supposed to do. Instead, it began on April 13, 2001, resulting in a variance of one day.

Figure 6–13 contains two other valuable indicators of project status. Did you notice the solid lines appearing on top of the striped bars? These bars represent the percent complete for each task. For example, for Task 9, *Research Competitors' Advertising Patterns* (abbreviated as *Res Compet Adver Paterns*) the solid bar has the same length as the striped bar, meaning the project is 100% complete, the striped bar representing planned task duration. Task 6, however, *Res Likely Branding Timeline*, stands only 33% complete, shown by the black bar being one-third the length of the striped bar.

The final piece of valuable information can be found in the lines that connect one task to another and end in an arrow. These lines indicate that one task is dependent on another. Task 9, for example, depends on the completion of Task 1. After all, how can Roy Johnson complete his task until he knows which competing catalogs to use for his research?

The fact that we know Task 9 is the responsibility of Roy Johnson highlights another tool *Project* brings to project management. *Project* allows a worker to be linked with one or several tasks.

never ending challenge

BESIDES ITS PROMISE of faster revisions, the movement to electronic project management reflects modern organizations' need to have fresh data. In part this stems from the cost of modern projects, particularly large projects. Another factor is the highly competitive nature of some industries. In those industries, a product's taking one year to design, market, and ship may compromise your company's market share.

Another factor is upper management's need to make decisions. Will the project really complete on time? When can we expect income from the new product? Are we overstaffed or understaffed for the projects we have next year?

Whether you report project status in Gantt or PERT or PERT/CPM or column charts, keep the questions in Figure 6-14 in mind.

Initial Question	Follow-Up Questions
What measurement does the project manager consider to be a warning sign?	Is it 15% over budget? 10% behind schedule?
What activities are considered critical?	Can you think of a fresh way to illuminate the status of critical path activities?
How fresh is your data?	Are you receiving contributions when you expect to receive them?
Is your data accurate?	Does your experience cause you to question data? Does the jump in percent completed seem too good to be true?

Initial Question	Follow-Up Questions
What format should your chart take?	If your project is routinely reported in Gantt charts, can you try a large, colorful bar chart to compare planned cost versus actual cost?
Are you interpreting data or only passing it on?	Do you see a pattern in the data your team has not discussed?

Figure 6-14: Gantt or PERT or PERT/CPM?

GLOSSARY

baseline—the original project plan in simplified form

critical path—a series of critical tasks

critical path method—a project management method that concentrates on preserving the schedule of the critical path

decision diagram—a flowchart that captures a decision-making process, including possible decisions and possible results

decision tree—a type of decision diagram that uses the tree metaphor (choices branch off into *yes* or *no* possibilities)

dependency—a relationship tying two tasks together

duration—the estimated amount of time required to complete a task

early finish—the earliest date the task will likely finish

early start—the earliest date the task will likely begin

finish-to-finish dependency—a dependency requiring one task to finish before another task can finish

finish-to-start dependency—a dependency requiring one task to finish before another task starts

fishbone diagram—a diagram using the metaphor of a fish skeleton to present the key factors contributing to a problem gantt chart—a chart that translates a series of start and end dates into horizontal bars representing duration

late finish—the latest date a task can finish and not delay the overall project deadline

late start—the latest date a task can begin and not delay the overall project deadline

PERT chart—a placing activities and events into a single framework, employing symbols and arrows to illustrate the sequential order of steps needed to complete a project

predecessor—a task that must complete before another task can complete

progress line—a line based on the status date showing tasks ahead of or behind schedule

pyramid chart—a chart using a pyramid shape to rank a series of values

resource—an asset that can be drawn upon to complete a project, usually staff and money

slack—(also called *float*) describes the time a task can be delayed before it becomes a critical task

start-to-finish dependency—a dependency requiring a second task to finish only after the first task starts

start-to-start dependency—a dependency requiring two tasks to start at the same time

status date—the date on which variances are based (e.g., as of this date, your task is three days behind schedule)

successor—a task that cannot complete without an action by another task

task—an individual piece of work that contributes to completion of a project

tree diagram—a diagram that branches out to show all possible outcomes or combinations

variance—the difference between the project plan and actual status

Ten Capabilities of the Electronic Gantt Chart

Electronic Gantt charts have dozens of options, tools, and views to help you create visual management tools. Here are ten capabilities to remember:

1. Comparing the percent of the project schedule that has been completed versus the amount of work that has been completed.
2. Comparing the cost and time a worker has charged against a project versus the cost and time allotted to that worker.
3. Comparing each task's current status with its baseline.
4. Creating a group of workers from which to draw resources.
5. Linking workers' names with their rate of pay (including overtime pay) and department.
6. Linking a task in one schedule with a task in another (so that changes in one changes the other).
7. Allowing contributors to submit their updates over the Internet.
8. Adding a recurring task to a project schedule so it appears regularly. and automatically (monthly status report due the 15th of each month).
9. Customizing the workweek of your workers. (Tuesday through Saturday? Ten hours per day?).
10. Zoom into a calendar focusing on a project period (e.g., three days) to offer a close up view of project activities.

▶▶▶ learning on your own

1. Draw a tree on a sheet of chart paper, and label it with a question that can be answered *yes* or *no*. Below the question, write *yes* on one side of the paper and *no* on the other. Under *yes*, list all the possible consequences of that decision. Do the same under *no*. Reach a decision based on the consequences. Can you explain why you reached that decision?

2. Why would a project be at risk if the project manager failed to track cost?

chapter
seven

Technical Drawings:
Blueprints, Whiteprints,
and Drawings

- ▶ **Blueprint**
- ▶ **Whiteprint**
- ▶ **Body**
- ▶ **Title block**
- ▶ **Revisions list**
- ▶ **Materials list**
- ▶ **Alphabet of lines**
- ▶ **Elevation**
- ▶ **Floorplan**
- ▶ **Land survey plat**
- ▶ **Site plan**

wonders around us

EACH DAY YOU walk or drive past modern marvels rivaling the Seven Wonders of the Ancient World. Buildings soar into the sky. Miles of concrete tubes carry underground trains and their thousands of bustling passengers. Airports handle hundreds of landings and takeoffs each day, as well as the tens of millions of passengers who flow through airport gates.

Have you considered how these marvels are built? For example, how does an army of cable and concrete layers, electricians, framers, masons, pipers, and

technical drawings **135**

telecommunications technicians know where to place the thousands of pieces that comprise a modern skyscraper? Well, they don't know. No one could. These craftspeople rely on detailed drawings to tell them what, when, how, how many, and what size.

Welcome to the complex and crucial world of technical drawings. They may not be the most dramatic pieces of visual communication, but without them, the modern world could not exist.

Chapter 7 offers a simple introduction to technical drawings, in part because creating these drawings requires specialized training. Consequently, the emphasis here lies on your understanding these drawings—creating them yourself. Still, whether you think you might want to pursue this vital branch of visual communication or your work requires occasional exposure to them, this chapter will guide you in deciphering these tried and true tools.

blueprints and whiteprints

BLUEPRINTS HAVE BEEN used to copy original architectural drawings since 1840. That was the year Sir John Herschel, an astronomer, invented the photographic blueprinting process. Blueprints are named *blueprints* because the blueprinting process creates documents with a Prussian blue background. The drawings themselves appear as white lines against the blue background.

In the work world, *blueprints*, *whiteprints*, *drawings*, and *prints* are often used interchangeably to describe copies made from original technical drawings. This chapter follows that custom.

Although they serve the same purpose, **whiteprints** (or *diazo prints*) have grown more popular than blueprints, in part because creating a whiteprint does not require treatment by liquids. Whiteprints feature a white background and black or colored lines.

Whether blue or white, technical drawings are legal documents. Many court actions have been decided by the weight of a blueprint. This is because drawings capture requirements, specifications, and processes.

> *Original* technical drawings require a considerable investment of time by a skilled technician. For this reason, original drawings are not taken to construction sites, factories, or machine shops where they could be damaged. Hence the need for blueprints and whiteprints.

If a dispute arises between parties (e.g., whether electrical outlets every six feet meet the owner's requirements), the blueprint answers:

- What was agreed to?
- When was it agreed to?
- Who agreed to it?
- When was the drawing complete?

It would be difficult to overstate the importance of drawings in the building and maintaining of our modern society.

parts of a blueprint/whiteprint

WHETHER IT ILLUSTRATES a single bolt or the ground floor of a new building, technical drawings consist of four basic sections, as illustrated in Figure 7-1:

- **Body**—the largest part of a technical drawing, the body contains the object being presented in the drawing; the body of the drawing also contains the notes added to explain and clarify the object.
- **Title block**—located in the lower right corner of the drawing, the title block contains fundamental information about the drawing (e.g., the name of the part shown, who created the drawing, who checked the drawing); Figure 7-2 shows a typical title block.
- **Revisions list**—also referred to as a revision block, the revision list appears in the upper right corner of a drawing; it contains data for each change made to the drawing (e.g., client requests, errors corrected, sub

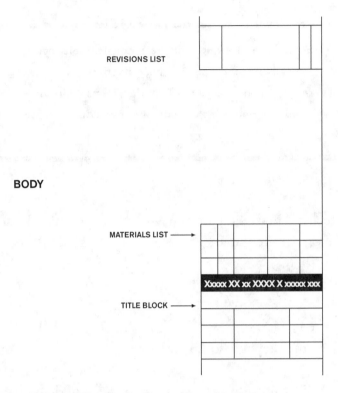

REVISIONS LIST

BODY

MATERIALS LIST ⟶

Xxxxx XX xx XXXX X xxxxx xxx

TITLE BLOCK ⟶

Figure 7-1: Basic pieces of a technical drawing

stituted materials); ample room must be left below the revisions list so that the list can be extended, if necessary.

- **Materials list**—commonly included on drawings illustrating more than one part, the materials list displays specific information on the materials used to create the key part (or key assembly) of the objects shown (some drawings include a separate parts list, while other drawings combine the materials and parts lists); the materials list sits just above the title block on the right of the drawing. Figure 7-1 shows where these sections are placed in a technical drawing.

body

Because it contains the object(s) being presented by the drawing, the body of a drawing is its largest part. In addition to an illustration of the object, the body often contains **notes** to help the reader understand important considerations or cautions. A note might contain:

- Spatial relationship between parts
- How tolerance will be measured
- Units of measurement in the drawing
- Issues that affect only a few parts

The area of a drawing containing title, scale, and date information is called a *title block;* the individual sections of a title block are also referred to as *blocks,* for example, *date block* or *scale block.*

---

the title block

The title block shown in Figure 7-2 belongs to a drawing used for manufacturing a part. A variation of this title block, however, could just as well be used for architectural drawings.

The following key describes the sections (sometimes called blocks) of a typical title block.

Key to Figure 7-2

1. Company name/company graphic—although technically not part of the title block, many companies place their company name or an identifying graphic somewhere in the title block to identify the drawing as their own.

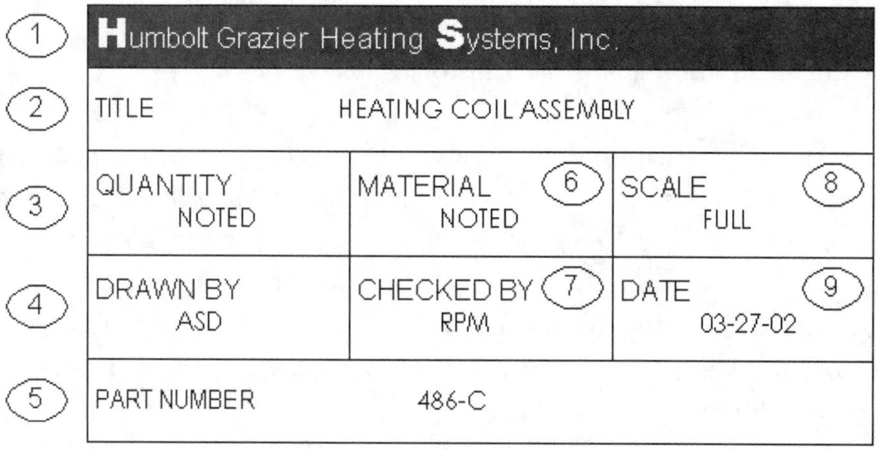

①	**H**umbolt Grazier Heating **S**ystems, Inc.		
②	TITLE	HEATING COIL ASSEMBLY	
③	QUANTITY NOTED	MATERIAL ⑥ NOTED	SCALE ⑧ FULL
④	DRAWN BY ASD	CHECKED BY ⑦ RPM	DATE ⑨ 03-27-02
⑤	PART NUMBER	486-C	

Figure 7-2: A typical title block for a manufacturing drawing

2. **Title**—the name of the object shown in the drawing.
3. **Quantity**—how many of the objects will be manufactured? In this case, the quantity has been shown somewhere else on the drawing, hence the use of *noted*.
4. **Drawn by**—the initials of the draftsperson.
5. **Part number**—the specific identification number of the part shown in the drawing; some part numbers are used as the drawing titles.
6. **Material**—the material used to make the part (e.g., tungsten steel) appears here; the word *noted* tells us that the material has been specified elsewhere in the drawing.
7. **Checked by**—the initials of the person who confirmed that the drawing was accurate and complete.
8. **Scale**—the relationship between the object as drawn and the actual object; the word *Full* tells us that the object is being shown full size or 1:1.
9. **Date**—when the drawing was completed.

revisions list

Because a variety of factors affect a project, a set of drawings soon becomes a set of revised drawings. Not all drawings are revised, of course, but multiple revisions of a single drawing are not uncommon. Prints are revised to:

- Provide accurate, current requirements to the people building and inspecting the project
- Maintain consistent quality and methodology
- Contain an unbroken project history

Because the information they illustrate often changes, because of their importance as project history, and because of their legal weight, revisions are carefully controlled. Before a revision is published, for example, a representative from each party commonly signs and dates the drawing and initials each change, thereby agreeing to the revision. The responsible parties might be the owner of a building (or her construction manager) and the company constructing the building.

Accurate drawings remain valuable even after a construction project ends. **As-builts** are drawings that describe a structure as it was actually built. As-builts are based on the finished structure, not on original design drawings. (As-builts may also be drawn of a long-completed structure, usually as a prelude to renovation.) Activities as diverse as repairing, maintaining, upgrading, and evacuating a building rely on as-builts.

Figure 7-3 shows a typical *Revisions* list, where revisions are tracked on a technical drawing.

Revisions cost money, which is one reason revisions are carefully tracked. For example, if a client requests a larger, nonstandard door for each entryway in a housing development, each drawing containing each entry door must be revised. Who pays for revising those drawings? (In this case, the client would.)

Key to Figure 7-3

1. **Revision number**—Every revision must be numbered (or lettered) to distinguish the revision from an original drawing on which it is based. For example, if the title for the Figure 7-1 drawing is Metal Screws 32-9, the first revised drawing might be Metal Screws 32-9 Rev. 1 or 32-9 (1) or 32-9-A. The method of indicating revisions remains secondary to the need for consecutive numbering.

2. **Description**—This is a very brief summary of the change that required a revised drawing; this information can save considerable time for someone looking for a particular change in a book of revised drawings.

	REVISIONS	③	④
NO.	DESCRIPTION ②	DATE	APPD.
1	TEFLON-COATED THREADS	02-22-02	NJP
2	SS 240 SPECIFIED	02-26-02	NJP

①

Figure 7-3: A typical revisions list for a manufacturing drawing

3. **Date**—This is the date the original drawing was changed, creating a revised drawing.
4. **Appd. (Approved)**—This indicates the initials of the person who approved the change.

materials list

A web of advisories, standards, regulations, and requirements determine the design of everything from bolts to jet engines. Requirements may be imposed by government agencies or the organization paying for the object to be manufactured or constructed. These requirements might specify levels of:

- Corrosion
- Cost
- Durability
- Ease of maintenance
- Environmental effect
- Reliability
- Safety
- Weight

To address these concerns, specific materials and parts are frequently required in manufacturing and construction. The **materials list** specifies what parts compose an assembly or what materials will be used to create an object, allowing a reviewer to verify that requirements have been met. Placing this information in a single location, as shown in Figure 7-4, allows reviewers to quicker review drawing.

Key to Figure 7-4
1. **Item number**—a sequential number identifying each object on a drawing; this number also appears beside the specific object it references.
2. **Quantity**—lists the number of items required to complete the part or assembly.

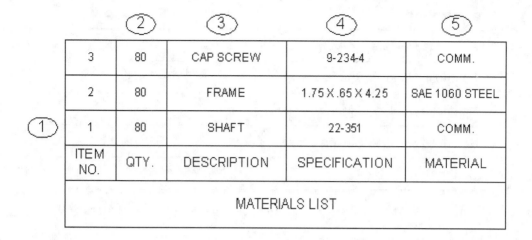

		②		③	④	⑤

ITEM NO.	QTY.	DESCRIPTION	SPECIFICATION	MATERIAL
3	80	CAP SCREW	9-234-4	COMM.
2	80	FRAME	1.75 X .65 X 4.25	SAE 1060 STEEL
1	80	SHAFT	22-351	COMM.

MATERIALS LIST

Figure 7-4: A typical materials list

3. Description—a brief note describing the object.

4. Specification—if the part will be manufactured, its size appears here (as in item 2); if the part will be purchased commercially, a manufacturer's stock number appears here.

5. Material—the material required to manufacture the part; if the part will be purchased commercially, the abbreviation *COMM.* appears here.

> While the revisions list resembles a typical table, the materials list resembles a table turned on its head—column headings are below, rather than above, the items in the column. This allows the materials list to be extended toward the top of the drawing (into the empty space under the revisions list) with minimal changes to the materials list, saving the title block from having to be moved.

drawing standards

WITH SO MANY industries around the world relying on technical drawings, you won't be surprised to learn that universal standards control many drawing characteristics. You might be surprised, however, to learn how far these

Organization	Abbreviation
American Institute for Architects	AIA
American National Standards Institute	ANSI
American Society of Mechanical Engineers	ASME
American Welding Society	AWS
United States Military	MIL*

*While not strictly an abbreviation for the United States military, MIL is often used this way (e.g., MIL specifications)

Figure 7-5: Organizations influencing drawing standards

conventions reach. Did you notice in Figure 7-2 that all the letters within the title block are upper case (TITLE)? This is only one voluntary standard used internationally.

Several organizations have considerable influence on drawing standards. Figure 7-5 lists five organizations (representing members who would likely create or use drawings) and their abbreviations.

measurement systems for drawings

BECAUSE DRAWINGS ARE used throughout the world, some base their dimensions on the **SI** (Système International) **measurement system**, also named *metric* system, while others use the **British/United States measurement system**. The metric system dominates science and engineering outside the United States. Many drawings display their dimensions in both systems. For engineering drawings based on the metric system, the *millimeter* is the unit of measure used most often. Drawings using the British/United States system commonly employ the *inch* and its fractions ($\frac{1}{8}, \frac{1}{4}, \frac{1}{3}, \frac{1}{2}, 1, 1\frac{1}{2}$) for dimensions.

drawing sizes

In describing large or complex objects, technical drawings often dwarf the size of most business documents. In fact, technical drawings may be the largest pieces of technical visual communication. Figure 7-6 shows standard sheet sizes for drawings, in both United States and SI dimensions.

Designation	Standard United States Size (inches)	Designation	Closest International Size (millimeters)
A	8.5 X 11.0	A4	210 X 297
B	11.0 X 17.0	A3	297 X 420
C	17.0 X 22.0	A2	420 X 594
D	22.0 X 34.0	A1	594 X 841
E	34.0 X 44.0	A0	841 X 1189

Figure 7-6: Standard sizes for drawings sheets

drawing scale

AN ESPECIALLY INTRICATE part might require a scale that represents the object in larger-than-actual size. Figure 7-7 shows common drawing scales.

Term	Decimal	Ratio
Full	1.00:1.00	1:1
Half	.50:1.00	1:2
Quarter	.25:1.00	1:4
Eighth	.125:1.00	1:8
Double	2.00:1.00	2:1
Triple	3.00:1.00	3:1

Figure 7-7: Terms commonly used in the scale block

technical drawings

When scales are shown in a title block, the first number in the ratio represents the drawing and the second number represents the actual object. So a ratio of 2:1 means the drawn object is twice as large as the actual object. Consequently, a ratio of 1:3 means the drawn object is one-third the size of the actual object.

drafting elements

DRAFTSPERSONS USE THE following elements to portray an object (or group of objects) clearly and accurately—a challenge considering that objects are 3-D and printed drawings are 2-D:

- **Dimensions**—indicate the size of individual objects or entire assemblies.
- **Geometric relationships**—preserve the spatial position between multiple objects (e.g., to show assembly instructions).
- **Lines**—combine with other lines to describe the shape of an object and its internal detail.
- **Notes**—nongraphical information that comments upon and explains the body of the drawing (e.g., all dimensions are centimeters).
- **Section views**—eliminate hidden lines and show internal detail; a **section view** presents an object as if it were sliced apart by a knife; the angle of the knife (horizontal, vertical) determines the section view.
- **Tolerances**—describe the accuracy required for shape, size, and position of surfaces when objects must meet high precision standards (e.g., 0.005 inch).
- **Views**—drawings for manufacturing common use multiple views of an object or group of objects to better explain their shape and proportion; these views are named **multiview** or **orthographic** drawings (you will learn more about views later in the chapter).

Many designers, planners, and architects now represent objects by using computer-aided design (CAD) illustrations rather than pen-and-ink drawings. CAD illustrations can bring a more lifelike, 3-D depiction of objects.

the alphabet of lines

MUCH AS A short story uses adjectives, adverbs, verbs, and nouns to describe a physical place, specific lines describe the object appearing in the body of a drawing. The lines typically found in a technical drawing are named the **alphabet of lines**. The alphabet consists of lines of varying thicknesses (fine, medium, heavy) and styles (broken, unbroken, dashes). As listed below and shown in Figure 7-8, this section explores five common lines from that alphabet.

- **Center lines**—fine lines consisting of alternating short and long dashes; center lines show the center point of an object; to clearly distinguish them from other lines, center lines extend beyond a shape.
- **Dimension lines**—fine, unbroken lines ending in arrowheads; dimension lines show the length of a measurement, see Figure 7-9.
- **Extension lines**—fine lines drawn perpendicularly to the dimension lines, indicating the limit of dimension lines.
- **Hidden lines**—medium lines composed of equal-length dashed lines; hidden lines indicate surfaces or intersections hidden by a shape.
- **Object lines (or visual lines)**—heavy lines defining the shape of an object by displaying the edges of its surfaces.

drawing views

ORTHOGRAPHIC DRAWINGS EMPLOY multiple views trying to overcome the paradox of illustrating a 3-D world on 2-D sheets of paper. One way to visualize how designers draw multiple views is by imagining the object in a glass box, as shown in Figure 7-10. Designers use **projectors**, imaginary lines of sight, to extend the object's image to one side of the glass box. This extended image is captured as a view. Now imagine that each projected image has been captured in each of the six sides of the glass box. Visualize the glass box opened and each glass side laid flat on a sheet of paper. Each glass side (with its image of the object) becomes a view. Figure 7-11 shows how designers display the unfolded box.

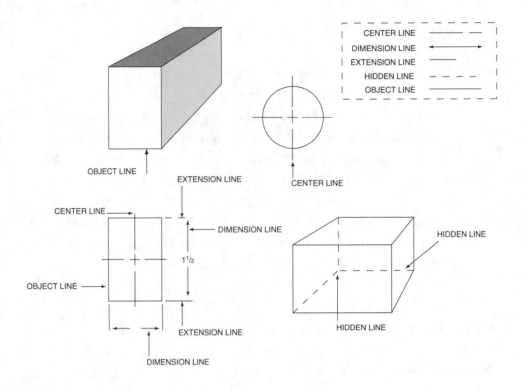

Figure 7-8: A sampling of five common lines used in technical drawings

The **principal views**, appearing in most multiview drawings, are the front, top, and right views. Describing some objects requires all six possible views— more than just the three principal views. Figure 7-11 presents the six possible views and shows their usual arrangement in a multiview technical drawing.

architectural drawings

ARCHITECTURAL DRAWINGS are the oldest form of technical drawings. In fact, architectural drawings have existed almost as long as recorded history and predate the invention of paper. A drawing from 2130 B.C., carved into a stone tablet, shows the layout of a temple.

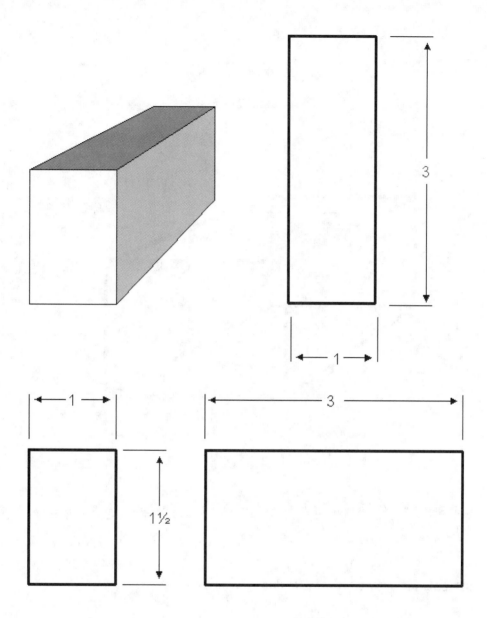

Figure 7-9: Dimension lines illustrate the size of an object

Frequently shown in architectural drawings, elevations (or *elevation views*) are equivalent to multiple views of an object in a manufacturing drawing. Four ground-level elevations are commonly used to illustrate structures: front, right, left, and rear.

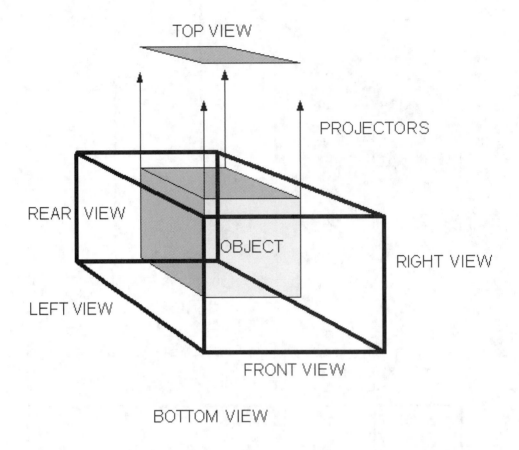

TOP VIEW

PROJECTORS

REAR VIEW

OBJECT

RIGHT VIEW

LEFT VIEW

FRONT VIEW

BOTTOM VIEW

Figure 7-10: Visualizing an object inside a glass box helps explain multiple views

symbols for architectural drawings

When you consider how many materials are used in structures—everything from brass to brick—it comes as no surprise that there are dozens of symbols used to add detail to architectural drawings. These symbols illustrate the range of metals, as well as depictions of natural materials, everything from clay to marble. Other symbols describe electrical and plumbing fixtures. Figure 7-12 offers a handful of these symbols, along with several floorplan conventions, by presenting a typical house floorplan. A **floorplan** is a section view showing the layout of a building as if a knife sliced through the building horizontally, midway between its floor and ceilings. Each floor of a structure has its own floorplan.

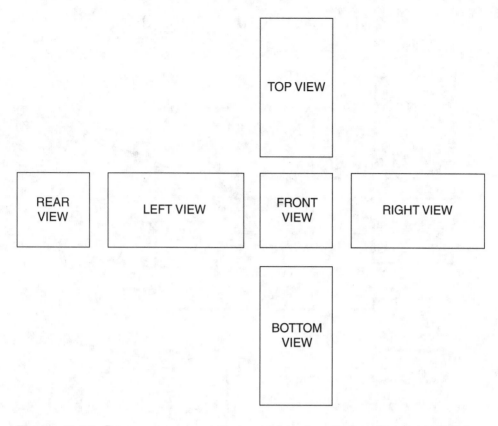

Figure 7-11: Proper arrangement of six possible views in an orthographic drawing

Key to Figure 7-12 (see next page)

1. A line shows the outline of a balcony.
2. Louvered window (windows that swing horizontally to open)
3. Sliding door
4. Junction of two walls
5. Fireplace
6. Stairs
7. Door (which closes flush with the wall and swings into the interior of a room)
8. Dimensions of the room (in feet and inches)
9. Door (folding, closet)
10. Kitchen sink
11. Kitchen range
12. Bathtub
13. Garage door

2410 LANDINGHAM, PARK RIDGE

Figure 7-12: This house floor plan uses only a few of the many
architectural drawing symbols

drawings of large areas

A **LAND SURVEY PLAT** is a drawing or map based on a land survey. Land survey plats are created for several reasons:

- To place the survey into public record
- To set the boundaries of a piece of property
- To gather information on a piece of land before development begins

A **site plan** presents an architect or planner's concept for an area—perhaps a housing development, a shopping center, or a recreational area. Figure 7-13 contains a typical site plan.

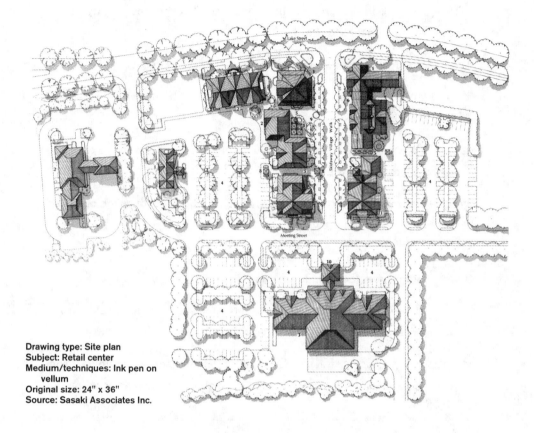

Drawing type: Site plan
Subject: Retail center
Medium/techniques: Ink pen on vellum
Original size: 24" x 36"
Source: Sasaki Associates Inc.

Figure 7-13: A typical site plan displays structures, parking, landscaping, and roads

alphabet of lines—a group of lines of varying thicknesses and styles typically found in technical drawings

as-built—a drawing describing a structure as it was actually built

blueprint—a copy of an original technical drawing; blueprints feature white lines on a blue background

blueprint reading—interpreting a blueprint so that you can visualize the object depicted in the drawing

body—the largest part of a technical drawing; the body contains the object being presented in the drawing

British/United States measurement system—a measurement system using yards, feet, and inches as units

center line—a fine line consisting of alternating short and long dashes; center lines show the center point of an object

computer-aided design (CAD)—formerly defined as computer-aided drafting; sometimes abbreviated as CADD (computer-aided design/drafting)

date block—a section of the title block that states when the drawing was completed and published; in a revisions list, the date block states the date the revision was made

dimension line—a fine, unbroken line (except where it is broken by a measurement) with arrowheads at each end; dimension lines show the length of a measurement

elevation—a view of a structure, as if it had been placed in a glass box; elevations usually consist of front, right, left, and rear ground-level views

extension line—fine line drawn perpendicularly to the dimension lines; extension lines indicate the limit of dimension lines floorplan—a section view showing the layout of a building as if a knife had sliced through the building horizontally, midway between its floor and ceiling

hidden line—a medium line composed of equal length dashed lines; hidden lines describe surfaces or intersections hidden by a shape

land survey plat—a drawing or map based on a land survey

materials list—the section of a drawing that lists the materials (or sometimes parts) needed to create or assemble the object shown in the drawing

note—a brief piece of text designed to help the reader better understand the drawing

object line—a heavy line showing the shape of an object

orthographic or multiview—a technical drawing using multiple views to describe an object

principal views—the front, top, and right views of an object

revisions list—the section of a drawing that contains each revision to the drawing

section view—a view designed to eliminate hidden lines and show internal detail; a section view presents an object as if it were sliced apart by a knife

site plan—an architect or planner's concept for an area

Système International (SI)—a measurement system based on the meter

title block—located in the lower right corner of the drawing, the title block contains fundamental information about the drawing

tolerance—a measurement of how much an object may vary (e.g., 0.005 inch)

whiteprint—a technical drawing printed with the Diazo process; whiteprints have grown more popular than blueprints

Ten Careers Using Technical Drawing Skills

The ability to create or interpret technical drawings touches many industries and occupations. Here are ten careers where this ability would give you a leg up.

Title	Skills
1. Apprentice	Basic craftsperson skills and understanding of tools and materials; ability to learn from experienced craftsperson
2. Architect	Highly imaginative person able to combine knowledge of construction, design, and site planning with artistic and problem-solving skills
3. Checker	Meticulous person with solid training in mathematics and sciences with emphasis in an architectural or engineering field (e.g., chemical, civil, electrical)
4. Craftsperson	Adept cabinet maker, carpenter, etc., with ability to produce individual parts and assemblies by using a variety of machines and tools
5. Designer	Person highly skilled in imaginative problem-solving; advanced skills in analyzing problems and creating solutions
6. Draftsperson	Understanding of mathematics and physics, as well as through practical knowledge of CAD/technical drawing; ability to work from engineer's drawings
7. Engineer	Solid training in mathematics and sciences with knowledge in a field of engineering (e.g., mechanical, structural)

8. Technicians	Highly trained in practical use of CAD principles, engineering, manufacturing requirements, and creation of prototypes
9. Technical Illustrator	Particularly skilled in visualizing 3-D objects from 2-D drawings; ability to produce a range of drawings for technical and marketing publications
10. Tracers	Basic skills in technical drawing and CAD; career ladder leads to draftsperson position after eight to twelve months of production experience

▶▶▶ **learning on your own**

1. Why do you think the title block includes a date block?

2. Why would some objects appearing in a drawing need to be shown in larger-than-actual-size scale?

3. What would be the value of illustrating a structure in four elevations?

4. In two columns, list the advantages and disadvantages of transmitting assembly instructions verbally rather than via a technical drawing.

From Circuits to Theaters:
Using Schematics

- ▶ **Schematic diagram**
- ▶ **Circuit**
- ▶ **Block diagrams**
- ▶ **Single line diagram**
- ▶ **Wiring diagrams**
- ▶ **Wire list**
- ▶ **Parts list**
- ▶ **Mechanical schematic**

deciphering electronics

A TECHNICIAN IN Taiwan assembles a computer video card. A computer designer in Texas studies a graphical representation of the same card as she decides which video card to install in her company's new computer product. A repair technician in Kansas searches for a reason a laptop computer's screen has gone black. Could it be a bad chip on the video card?

Each of these expert technicians uses a **schematic diagram** (sometimes referred to as *schematics*) to decipher the workings of an electronic device. The

Taiwanese technician speaks no English and the repairperson in Kansas speaks no Chinese. With the reliance of the modern world on similar devices (e.g., automobiles, computers, home entertainment equipment), these devices must be described through a method of visual communication that transcends languages, cultures, and locations. Schematics do that.

Schematics has also come to mean diagrams or layouts in fields other than electronics. These other schematics will be addressed near the end of this chapter.

schematic diagrams

FOR ELECTRICAL EQUIPMENT, a schematic shows the function of a piece of equipment and how the equipment accomplishes its purpose. For example, a schematic diagram might display the parts of a smoke alarm and how electricity flows through the parts to detect smoke and set off an alarm. An electrical schematic describes how multiple components are connected to act as a whole. Figure 8-1 shows a very simple but complete schematic: An electrical circuit composed of a single-cell battery and one lamp. A **circuit** is a closed path linking a power source and components; current flows from the power source through the components and back to the power source.

Despite its simplicity, the Figure 8-1 schematic employs several standard symbols to tell its electrical story. Figure 8-2 describes those symbols.

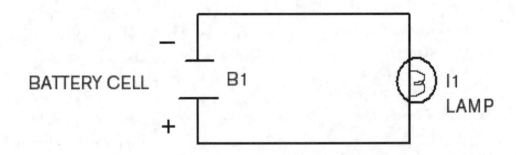

Figure 8-1: A simple schematic for a simple electrical circuit
Source: This image is excerpted from *Schematic Diagrams: The Basics of Interpretation and Use,*
by J. Richard Johnson.

Symbol	Meaning
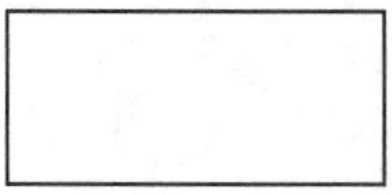	Represents an electrical connection between the battery and lamp; a straight line between two devices shows they are connected.
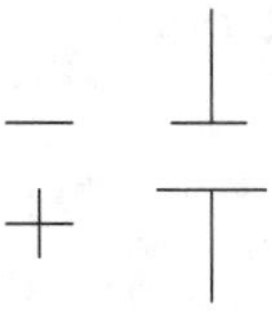	The symbol for a one-cell battery.
	The symbol for a lamp.
B1	The letter symbol for a battery (B); can also be written B_1; the number following the (B) tells us this is the first battery in the schematic; if another battery was added to the schematic, it would be designated B2.
I1	The letter symbol for a lamp (I); can also be written I^1

Figure 8-2: Symbols found in Figure 8-1

A schematic of a electrical device, as shown in Figure 8–1, analyzes the necessary components of a piece of equipment and presents those components graphically. The schematic shows negative charges flowing from the negative terminal of the battery, through the lamp, and returning to the positive terminal of the battery, completing the circuit. The power source usually appears on the left and the devices using that power are placed on the right in an electrical schematic.

Although schematics can be classified as technical drawings, they certainly differ from the technical drawings you explored in Chapter 7. You have possibly spotted several differences already. Let's examine Figure 8-1 more closely to better understand those differences.

Electrical schematics are usually read from left to right and top to bottom.

Unlike a whiteprint, the schematic in Figure 8-1 offers no:

- Unit of measurement; this is a clue that schematics are unconcerned with physical size
- Multiple views of the same device, as orthographic drawings have
- Spatial relationship between components (Is the battery directly across the circuit from the lamp? Perhaps. Perhaps not.)
- Description of the wire used to complete the circuit (Is it made of copper or platinum? How thick is it?)
- Description of the size or type of the lamp (Does it use an incandescent or halogen bulb?)
- Description of the size of the battery (True, we know the battery has only one cell—a pretty basic battery—but how much power does it provide?)

Why doesn't an electrical schematic include multiple views or component materials the way drawings do?

To provide information in a clear way, electrical schematics jettison everything that does not contribute to their mission, which is representing how a device functions electrically. This is particularly important because electrical schematics frequently represent complex pieces of equipment. Notice in Figure 8-1 that the line connecting the battery and the lamp allows enough room for the symbols, with little extra space. Conserving space allows room for other components to be added without clutter.

If two components in an electrical schematic are not connected by a straight line, the components are not connected in the actual circuit.

Schematics are often bound in books for distribution; therefore, conserving space means more information can be presented on a single page. Finally, schematics are often used in the field by technicians who may not have the luxury of tables and counter tops to spread out large drawings.

To remain compact, while also remaining clear, electrical schematics use straight lines, with rare exceptions, to connect electrical components. This is because straight lines are the shortest and simplest route between two points. To reduce the number of lines crossing each other, the great majority of lines in an electrical schematic are horizontal or vertical. Lines meet in 90-degree corners, and multiple lines traveling in the same direction are often grouped to conserve space.

Compare the use of space in Figure 8-1 to the use of space in Figure 8-3.

Each component in an electrical schematic has its own symbol. (See Figure 8-5 on pages 165-166 for a list of common symbols.) The symbols for electrical components vary somewhat, however, depending on the type of illustration being created. For instance, symbols may vary among a working drawing, a schematic, and a wiring diagram. Within a single drawing, however, the symbol for lamp (shown in Figure 8-2) is the same whether it describes a streetlamp or a flashlight bulb.

Symbols sharing a common function are grouped together in a schematic. For example, the symbol for the on/off switch might be placed beside the computer's power source, to which the on/off switch is logically linked. The actual on/off switch, however, might be many inches from the power source. There is a reason for the disparity between the electrical schematic's description of a device and the device's actual physical arrangement.

Some electrical schematics do not show the source of power energizing the circuit.

Because an electrical schematic limits itself to a device's function, not its actual size or layout, one schematic may stand for several configurations of components. Figure 8-4 shows three configurations of the components shown in Figure 8-1.

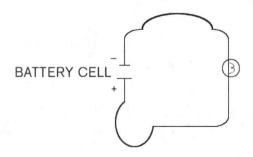

BATTERY CELL

Figure 8-3: A less compact schematic diagram

Figure 8-4: Figure 8-1's schematic represents any of these physical arrangements
Source: This image is excerpted from *Schematic Diagrams: The Basics of Interpretation and Use*,
by J. Richard Johnson.

Figure 8-5 displays a number of the most common symbols found on electrical schematics and defines the components they represent.

Symbol	Component	Definition
 ─(~)─	Alternator	A device to produce alternating current
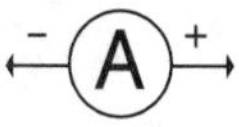 ─(A)+	Ammeter	An electric meter used to measure current in amperes
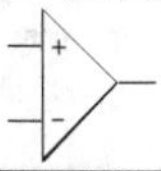 ─▷+ −	Amplifier	A device enabling an input signal to directly control a larger energy flow
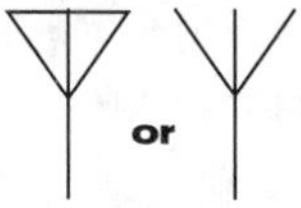 Y or Y	Antenna	A device for reception or transmission of electromagnetic waves
 ─⌒─	Circuit breaker	A resettable fuse-like device designed to protect a circuit against overloading
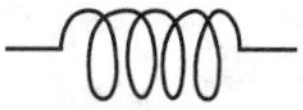 ─○○○○─	Coil	A cable or wire wound in a series of closed loops
 ─< → **Female** **Male** **GF** **GM**	Connector	A device used to physically and electrically connect at least two conductors
 (F)	Fan	An axial or radial flow device used for producing artificial currents of air
 ─○∿○─	Fuse	A protective device whichopens a circuit when the fusible element is severed by heating, due to too much current passing through
 ─(GEN)─	Generator	A rotating machine which converts mechanical energy to electrical energy
 ⏚	Ground (Earth)	A large conductive body (for example, the Earth) used as acommon return for an electric current
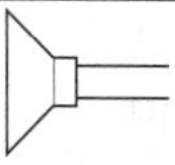 ◁	Loud speaker	Equipment that converts an electric signal into an acoustic signal

Figure 8-5: Common electronic/electrical schematic symbols and their definitions

Symbol	Component	Definition
(MOT)	Motor	An apparatus that converts electrical energy to mechanical energy
	117 Volt Plug	A male connector that inserts into an outlet
O	Receptacle	A contact device installed at the outlet to connect a plug
▶	Rectifier	A device to change alternating (Semi conductor) current to single-direction current
⌇	Resistor	A device whose primary purpose is to introduce resistance
⟋	Switch	A device for opening/closing or (single-pole) for changing the connection of a circuit
⊶	Terminals (balanced)	Devices for connecting cables.
⧙	Transformer (iron-core)	A static device made of windings, for introducing mutual coupling by induction between circuits

Figure 8-5 (*continued*)

block diagrams

A VALUABLE TOOL for the development of products or designs, **block diagrams** capture only the essential components of a piece of equipment. Because of their focus on the essential, block diagrams are often considered the most elementary form of electronic drawings. Of course, their simplicity (refer to Figure 8-6) makes them easy to revise and present, valuable features for an engineer in the early stages of product design.

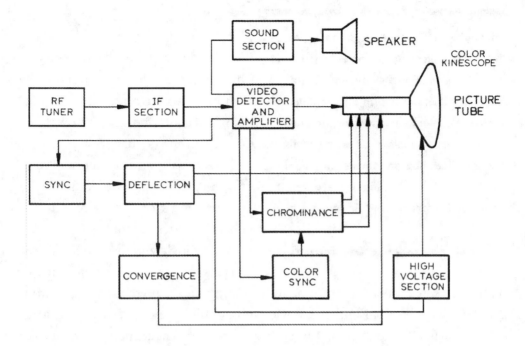

Figure 8-6: A basic block diagram describing a simple color television receiver
Source: This image is excerpted from *Electronics Drafting*, by John R. Frostad.

Using fewer symbols than an electrical schematic, block diagrams are probably the easiest diagrams for nontechnicians to understand. Because many readers are familiar with flow diagrams or organization charts, they are able to decipher the similar construction of a block diagram. In fact, you probably have seen block diagrams used in sales brochures to describe the features of an electronic product. If you are preparing a presentation of the ideas behind your company's new electronics product to a range of managers in your company, a block diagram would communicate your message better than a schematic.

As shown in Figure 8-6, a block diagram of a simple color television receiver, lines or arrows connect the components, displayed as blocks. A block often represents multiple parts, as it does here, where one block symbolizes the multi-component RF tuner (RF is the abbreviation for radio frequency; IF is the abbreviation for intermediate frequency). The arrows show the path of the signal or energy within the device. In Figure 8-6, for example, the signal travels from the RF tuner to the IF section to the video detector and amplifier. Here the signal branches off in two directions. The signal travels to the sound section and then to the speaker. In one flow, signal also travels from the video

After a block diagram has been approved, the next step in designing an electrical product is often creating a single line diagram. A single line diagram, a form of schematic, describes the interconnections of components using varying line thicknesses and symbols. A single line diagram shows only enough detail to describe the general layout of the circuit, but offers more detail than a block diagram.

detector and amplifier to the picture tube. Notice that the picture tube and the speaker are represented by symbols, while the rest of the components are represented by rectangles common to most flowcharts or organization charts.

Block diagrams sometimes refer to a further description of the block's requirements or design or unusual characteristics. Figure 8-7 shows a sample block with a number, 3, referring to an engineer's note, perhaps on how selective the tuner must be in separating one radio station's signal from another. A block representing a power supply might refer the reader to a requirement that the power supply be low power or that it must automatically adapt to North American or European current.

wiring diagrams

TO SUMMARIZE, electrical schematics provide a simple representation of a circuit, and a block diagram presents a piece of equipment's essential components. However, the workers who construct and install electrical systems require more precise information. Their primary concern may not be troubleshooting, but rather building a system that meets the engineer's requirements and the client's needs. **Wiring diagrams** address the concerns of those workers. Figure 8-8 compares a simple wiring diagram (A) with a simple electrical schematic (B).

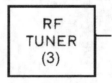

Figure 8-7: A block with a reference designation

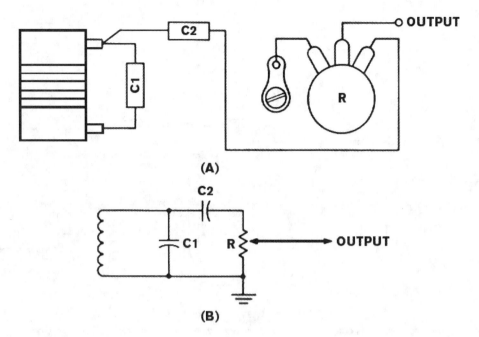

Figure 8-8: A wiring diagram and electrical schematic have different goals
Source: This image is excerpted from *Schematic Diagrams: The Basics of Interpretation and Use*,
by J. Richard Johnson

Wiring diagrams show actual connections between electrical components, including a representation of a component's place on the physical layout of the circuit. This is crucial because the order of connections matter. If a component does not connect to a circuit in the correct way, it may not work.

The more complex wiring diagram depicts an electrical distribution system for a recreational vehicle trailer park. Unlike a schematic or block diagram, this wiring diagram in Figure 8-9 notes the amount of electricity running through elements of the circuit. Figure 8-10 defines several common abbreviations for units of measure found in wiring diagrams.

Draftspersons commonly help technicians read wiring diagrams by creating a wire list and a parts list. A wire list describes the wires used in the wiring diagram, including the color of the wire, its length, and its thickness. The parts list, similar to a drawing's materials list, describes the nature and quantity of parts required to complete the equipment.

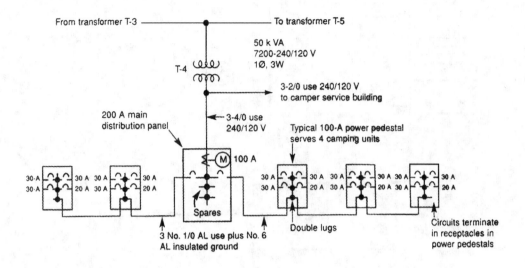

Figure 8-9: A wiring diagram

Source: This image is excerpted from the *Illustrated Guide to the 1999 National Electrical Code* by John E. Traister, revised and updated by Bradford Maher.

Abbreviation	Unit	Definition
A	Ampere	The basic SI unit that measures the quantity of electricity
k	Kilo-	Prefix meaning a *thousand* (kilogram, kilometer, kilowatt)
V	Volt	The derived SI unit for voltage: One volt equals one watt per ampere
VA	Volt-Ampere	Unit of electrical measure equal to the product of a volt x ampere that for direct current constitutes a measure of power equivalent to a watt
W	Watt	The SI measurement of electrical power, equal to 1/746 horsepower

Figure 8-10: Abbreviations for units of measure commonly found in wiring diagrams

standards

CHAPTER 7 LISTED a handful of organizations that significantly influence the creation of technical drawings and the objects they represent. The National Electrical Code (NEC) similarly influences electrical construction. Dating from 1897, the NEC is periodically revised to incorporate changing conditions, materials, and hazards. Now published by the National Fire Protection Association (NFPA), the NEC seeks to protect people and property from the hazards inherent in the potent power of electricity. The NEC addresses electrical components in everything from appliances to recreational vehicles, illustrating the number of electrical devices in our lives.

For example, an architect designing an airplane hanger will find NEC requirements for placing light receptacles within the hanger. NEC requirements specify that a technician installing a motor must install the motor's disconnect switch within sight of the motor and not more than 50 feet away.

If you are contemplating a career in electrical engineering, working with electrical schematics, or working in electrical construction, a knowledge of the latest edition of the NEC will serve you well.

Underwriters Laboratories (UL) and National Electrical Manufacturers Association (NEMA) also contribute to electrical standards. UL, a laboratory independent of manufacturers, tests electrical devices and focuses on user safety. NEMA standards, on the other hand, are often cited in construction procedures.

nonelectrical uses of schematics

SCHEMATIC DIAGRAMS ARE now employed to describe objects far different from electric circuits. Figure 8-11 shows the design of an arena theater (sometimes called a *theater in the round*), in which the audience sits around the stage, not just before it. The dark, gray circle at the center of the schematic represents the stage. It is immediately encircled by a white ring, symbolizing an aisle. Represented by ever widening rings are the first sections of seats (shown by broken, gray circles), another aisle, and then other sections of seats.

Figure 8-11: Schematic drawing of an arena theater

Rather than showing the necessary electrical components of a piece of equipment, a **mechanical schematic** analyzes the necessary mechanical components of a piece of equipment and represents how those components function in the whole. Figure 8-12, for example, shows the necessary parts of a cable reel, which is used to pull electrical cable through a trench. Mechanical schematics often elaborate on how a piece of equipment should be operated. For the schematic shown in Figure 8-12, someone operating the cable reel would need to know that he or she needs to turn the reel counter-clockwise to pull the cable through the trench in a counter-clockwise rotation.

Schematics often make their way into other forms of technical drawings. A wiring diagram of the electrical receptacles and lamps within a suite of offices is often superimposed upon a floorplan of the offices. A modified schematic might include illustrations of the actual lamps used in an installation. Whatever their form, schematics must be clear pieces of visual communication, accessible to craftspeople and technicians, and they must use a clear vocabulary of symbols, abbreviations, and notes.

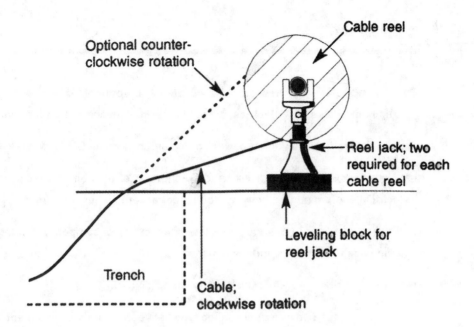

Figure 8-12: A mechanical schematic

Source: This image is excerpted from the *Illustrated Guide to the 1999 National Electrical Code* by John E. Traister, revised and updated by Bradford Maher.

block diagram—captures only the essential components of a piece of equipment; the easiest electrical drawing for nontechnicians to understand

circuit—a closed path linking a power source and components

schematic diagram (schematics)—shows the function of a piece of electrical equipment and how the equipment accomplishes its purpose

single line diagram—describes the interconnections of components using varying line thicknesses and symbols

wire list—describes the wires used in the wiring diagram

wiring diagram—shows actual connections between electrical components, including a representation of a component's place on the physical layout of the circuit

mechanical schematic—analyzes the necessary mechanical components of a piece of equipment and represents how those components function in the whole

POWER OF 10

Where Is My Schematic?

Because this chapter concentrates on schematics and diagrams as helpful tools for creating, building, and installing electrical components and equipment, you probably see the value of these drawings for electrical engineers. But have you considered how many other fields routinely use schematics?

1. Interior Design
2. Physics
3. Firefighting
4. Radio Construction
5. Aerospace Technology
6. Construction Planning
7. Airplane Maintenance
8. Special Events Planning
9. Robotics
10. Geology

 learning on your own

1. You are an electrical engineer asked to design a new product for your company. What diagram(s) would you likely use to commit your ideas to paper?

2. When might a schematic be preferable to a wiring diagram?

3. Why do you think there is sometimes more than one symbol for electric components?

chapter
nine

Navigating the Computer World

- **Personal computer**
- **Graphical user interface (GUI)**
- **Root folder**
- **Subfolder**
- **Icon**
- **Toolbar**
- **Personal data assistants**
- **Pictograms**

the perplexing genie

IMAGINE YOURSELF AT work, wondering how you will cut through the pile of assignments on your desk. There are invoices to balance and letters to type and a chart to create, if you can find the time to take it to the graphic artist down the hall. You rub your eyes. When you open them, a large green man towers over your desk. He seems friendly and looks like a character from the story of Aladdin. Could he be a genie?

He motions to your paperwork, but when he speaks you cannot understand a word he says. He cannot understand anything you say; even your hand motions fail to communicate.

Feel lost? Frustrated that you cannot unlock the power of your personal genie? That describes how computer users felt in the early 1970s.

a visual communication problem

IN THE EARLY 1970s, computers were becoming smaller and more powerful, but no product yet existed that was as popular as today's personal computers. There was also no *must-have* application—a product that was so desirable that buyers would live with a computer's idiosyncrasies just to have the advantages of that application. In 1976, when the Apple computer was introduced, there was a must-have program waiting to run on it—*Visicalc*, the granddaddy of all spreadsheet programs. The market for the personal computer expanded.

When IBM introduced the IBM PC in 1981, demand swelled. Computer owners watched a race between hardware and software—new hardware brought great speed and capacity, while new software absorbed that speed and capacity with new features. But as this race zoomed past one milestone after another, one lingering barrier remained: creating a method for users to communicate more easily with these stubborn machines. After all, even the personal computer of the early 1980s was little better than the family cat at telling its owner it was ailing.

Humans interpret colors and words and sounds. Computers don't. Computers recognize the *binary system*, the only form of communication they understand. The binary system consists of two numbers: 1 and 0. For example, when you type the letter *B*, your computer sees 01100010.

This chapter uses the term **personal computer (PC)** to define a computer generally used by a single operator; a computer complete with keyboard and monitor, its own operating system (whether Macintosh or *Windows*), and the ability to use a variety of software applications.

Suddenly, the widespread use of the personal computer became an issue of visual communication. For the personal computer to free information from the refrigerator-sized mainframes and deliver that information to the fingertips of workers, those workers must understand how to manipulate that information—without having studied computer science. And if the computer industry couldn't give their creations a clear, colorful—even friendly face—how could they expand their market from the workplace to the average home?

graphics to the rescue

So, BEGINNING WITH Apple Corporation's introduction of the Macintosh in 1984, and later with Microsoft's introduction of *Windows 1.0* in 1985, the two significant operating system producers tried to rescue their users. Instead of typing odd commands in white letters on a harsh, black screen, users would be able to interact with a **graphical user interface** (GUI).

A GUI offers color buttons, menus, boxes, and a mouse to click on them— all an attempt to organize the many commands required to run an application. This, Apple and Microsoft hoped, would save users from having to remember nonsensical groups of letters and symbols. The GUI programmers tried to explain a computer by incorporating real-world objects, such as pages or graph paper or Gantt charts or rulers. By requiring other software companies to incorporate the GUI into their own products—or risk alienating Macintosh and Windows customers—Apple and Microsoft standardized the basic way users accessed applications.

who is training whom?

UNFORTUNATELY, PERSONAL COMPUTERS confound our expectations. Compared to the human brain, computers cannot infer, extrapolate, or use instinct. In many ways, personal computers are very fast, yet very dumb. And unlike a microwave oven or a fan, a personal computer performs a great many tasks, compounding its communication problems. Ironically, instead of users training the computers, the computer's GUI trains the users. In this way, personal computers and the interface that allows humans to access them are a tremendous force for training—human training.

Fortunately, visual communication can help bridge this gap between human and machine. We will see how visual communication does this as we explore a key, but sometimes murky, question: How do I find my data?

understanding structure and hierarchy

A PERSONAL COMPUTER strains our ability to understand its logic because the numbers connected with computing are so large. A new personal computer with a huge hard disk has the capacity to store *millions* of pieces of correspondence. If you are new to computing, you may succumb to temptation and store your letters or charts or spreadsheets anywhere and everywhere on your hard disk. After all, the storage space seems so huge, what does it matter? This complacency, however, is the road to ruin. Eventually, you will need to recover those documents you created. If you are less than systematic about storing your work, you may be searching for a very long time.

Figure 9-1 illustrates one way to conceive of a personal computer's hard disk, as a large tree.

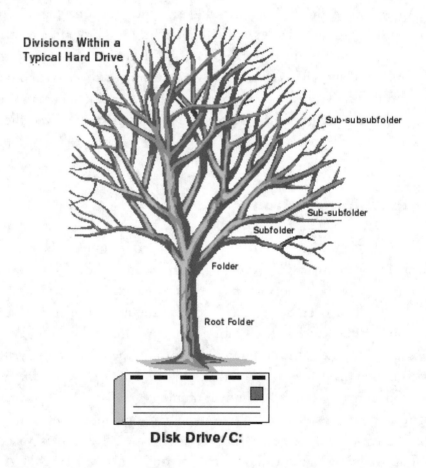

Figure 9-1: A tree is the metaphor often used to explain a hard disk's organization

Imagine your hard disk as a rich patch of ground and from that patch grows a tree. The trunk of the tree is the **root folder**, a folder that usually holds no data itself, a folder named after the drive it belongs to (e.g., C). Although the root folder rarely holds data, it holds other folders, named **subfolders**. In the hard disk's hierarchy, a subfolder falls under a folder. A subfolder can have a sub-subfolder under it and so on and so on. Some computer users find it easier to have only a few folders, equivalent to a few main branches on a tree. Other users create many folders and subfolders—equivalent to many large and medium branches on a tree; they use this structure to organize their work.

You can create as many folders as you like on a hard disk or floppy disk without reducing the remaining space on your disk.

However, no matter what structure you design—complex or simple—the goal is to easily find the files you need within their appropriate folders. Another metaphor to explain the drive/folder/file hierarchy of computer storage relies on the common experience of using a file cabinet, represented in Figure 9-2.

Figure 9-2: A file cabinet can be used to explain the organization of a hard disk

Think of your hard disk as the drawer of a filing cabinet in the Grainville Baking Company headquarters office. You are assigned to locate the invoices sent to catering customers in January 2002. Figure 9-3 compares the actions you would take to find the information in the real world versus finding the information in your PC.

Real World		Computer World	
Step	Action	Step	Action
1	Open the drawer	1	Double-click on the drive
2	Search for the correct folder	2	Search for the correct folder
3	Open the correct folder	3	Double-click on the folder
4	Search for the correct file	4	Search for the correct file
5	Pull the file from the folder	5	Double-click on the file
6	Search the file for the information	6	When the application opens the file, search the file for the information

Figure 9-3: The steps for finding a file are similar in the real and computer worlds

Now we will concentrate on building a folder structure in the computer world. You can create as many folders as you find necessary in the structure that works best for you. Figure 9-4 illustrates two methods of structuring the same information. Structure A organizes invoices by year (to conserve space, Figure 9-4 only shows the 2002 folder) and then by the months of 2002. Structure B organizes invoices under the year they were issued and then separates them based on whether they pertain to income or expenses. Structure B then breaks down the expenses further by the type of income or expense they pertain to.

As you may guess, chaos results when the structure of a hard disk resembles structure C. True, documents are broken down by year. But after each year a single folder follows, which will soon become a grab bag of various files created by various applications; in short, a filing disaster.

Some computer users name folders after the application that created the file. So, for example, one major folder might be named *WordPerfect* Files or *AutoCAD* Files.

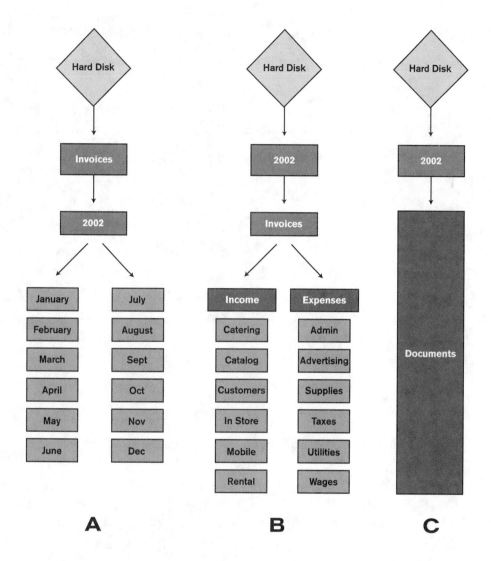

Figure 9-4: A and B are effective ways to organize the same data;
C is a filing disaster

Now that you have seen (or reviewed) the importance of structuring your hard disk wisely, let's see how an application displays the folders and files stored on a PC. In *Microsoft Windows*, a frame within a window is called a **pane**. Figure 9-5 displays a section of a hard disk in the left pane of the window. Notice that the application in Figure 9-5 uses an *icon* of a folder to represent each folder and subfolder. An **icon** is an image that resembles what it represents. Icons, when clicked on, perform tasks without the user having to select a command from a menu or type a command on a keyboard.

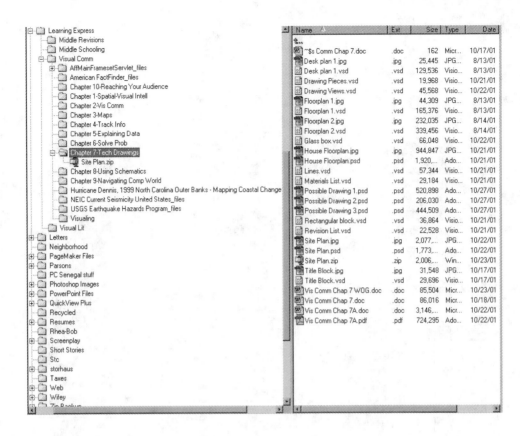

Figure 9-5: The folder tree growing in its real environment

For example, if you double–click on a folder icon with a plus sign beside it (+), the folder opens to reveal its subfolders. This is what happened to the *Visual Comm* folder in Figure 9-5. When the folder expands, its plus sign disappears to be replaced with a minus sign (-). The minus sign indicates that all subfolders have been revealed. So, how does Figure 9-5 aid us in finding a file? The left pane shows a folder named *LearningExpress*. The computer user has expanded that folder and revealed four subfolders:

- Middle Revisions
- Middle Schooling
- Visual Comm
- Visual Lit

The computer user has expanded one of those four subfolders: *Visual Comm*. Under Visual Comm are 16 folders. Notice that the icon for one folder, *Chapter 7-Tech Drawings*, features a different icon. Its icon represents an open folder, rather than a closed folder. The open folder icon indicates that the contents of the *Chapter 7-Tech Drawings* folder are displayed in the right pane.

Suppose you had been looking for a single file, *Site Plan.jpg*, a graphics file. That file is clearly displayed in the right pane. All you need to do is double-click on the icon beside the file name. The application that created the file will open, displaying the file you selected.

After you create a logical hierarchy of folders, remember to be diligent about where you save files. For instance, if you have a folder named *July Correspondence*, make sure you save all July correspondence to that folder. If not, you will find yourself with duplicate files: Those you saved in the correct folder and those you saved somewhere else. Eventually, you have to spend time comparing files to discover which ones to retain.

There is another set of icons at play in Figure 9-5. *Microsoft Windows* reminds you of the application used to create a file by placing an icon representative of the application beside the file name. Highlighting a section of the right pane appearing in Figure 9-5, Figure 9-6 displays several of those application icons.

To best track your files, avoid saving them in broadly named folders. For example, in structure A of Figure 9-4, avoid saving files in the *2002* folder. When you return months later, the file name may not reawaken your memory. A file saved in the *Dec* folder under the *2002* folder, however, already prompts you on the subject of the file. Ideally, folders such as *2002* should only contain folders, not files.

American FactFinder.htm	An HTML file created to be used on the web
arrow92.jpg	A .jpg file (a compressed graphics file)
Drew's M&Ms.xls	An *Excel* workbook file
House Floorplan.psd	A *Photoshop* file (*Photoshop* creates and edits graphics files)
Invoices	A what file? Windows does not recognize the application that created this file. (Notice the file has no file extension, such as .xls.) If you double-click on this file, Windows will ask you to select an application to open the file.
Practice.xls	An Excel workbook file (notice the *X* on the icon)
Psd3.psd	*Photoshop* file (notice the *.psd* extension)
Signs1.psd	*Photoshop* file (notice the *.psd* extension)
Vis Comm 7-30-01 Out.doc	A *Word* file (notice the *W* on the icon)

Figure 9-6: These icons remind you of the application used to create each file

Today's personal computer applications feature icons everywhere, part of software manufacturers' efforts to provide users direct access to the features they use most often. Figure 9-7 shows the *toolbars* that appear in *PowerPoint XP* when you first open the application. Microsoft calls a collection of icons (each representing a tool or function) a **toolbar**. In many applications, toolbars and their icons can be added or replaced by the user.

Figure 9-7: *PowerPoint XP's* opening screen features a single, icon-rich toolbar

---

Icons not only act as representatives of functions, they also act as placeholders. After using an icon for a while, users naturally head their mouse button to the section of the screen containing the icon.

---

personal data assistants

DURING THE LAST several years, *personal data assistants* (PDAs) have grown to be an extremely popular segment of the personal computer market. Although not as powerful as full-sized personal computers, **PDAs** offer users the ability to take personal information everywhere with them: Data such as telephone numbers, to do lists, addresses, and notes. An abbreviated keyboard, appearing on the PDAs screen, even allows the user to enter notes. Through the use of a cable, PDAs can synchronize their information with a desktop or laptop personal computer, allowing its owner to ensure he or she always has the latest information nearby.

Because PDAs must offer a variety of options within a limited screen, and because one of their selling points is ease of use, PDAs rely on a number of icons. Figure 9-8 shows a popular PDA, the Palm™ m505, and a group of its icons.

Did you notice that the PDA's screen repeats several of the icons appearing in Figure 9-8? Did you notice that the icons appearing on the screen are labeled?

icons everywhere

IF ICONS ARE so prevalent in the computer world, they have become important pieces of visual communication and worthy of some exploration here. Of course, icons appear around us each day, even if we never turn on a computer.

Battery power remaining

Find and open applications

Scroll

Calculator

Find a name or word

Access the datebook

Access addresses

Access a To Do list

Enter data

Figure 9-8: This personal data assistant (PDA) relies heavily on icons

They caution us about road conditions or the location of a restroom. They communicate the heritage of a religion and warn us of hazardous work conditions. They indicate where we can safely ride our bicycles and warn us of poison.

The study of signs is called **semiotics**, which includes the study of icons and symbols throughout recorded time. Without delving too far into the world of semiotics, icons—particularly types of icons and why they communicate so well—are the focus here.

ancient tools with new life

ICONS PREDATE THE written word. When ancient peoples wanted to describe something, they drew it. A written language only became necessary to express complex or abstract thoughts. Although icons have existed through history, the end of the 19th century signaled their renaissance as a tool to communicate with people who spoke different languages. This need grew from increased travel. In fact, the western world's first road signs were not created by a government agency, but by the Italian Touring Club in 1895. The first international road signs began appearing in 1909. Increased international travel after World War I emphasized the need for signs everyone could understand and sent graphic designers looking for solutions.

Those designers rediscovered a form of icon is called a *pictogram*. **Pictograms** are drawn or painted images that stand for a word or phrase. *Pictogram* combines two ancient words: *Pictus*, the Latin word meaning *painted*, and *gramma*, a Greek word meaning *writing*. You can probably guess that pictograms are a time-tested form of communication. Some of the hieroglyphs that graced Egyptian temples were pictograms. Pictograms come in three varieties, as shown in Figures 9-9, 9-10, and 9-11.

- **Abstract**—These images don't reference an object; instead, they are part of a code understood by an audience long exposed to the code. A visitor from another culture may find abstract pictograms unfathomable.

Figure 9-9: An abstract pictogram representing nuclear radiation

- **Figurative**—These images represent the object or activity they reference.

Figure 9-10: A figurative pictogram

navigating the computer world **189**

- **Schematic**—These images rely on a very general outline of the word or phrase being represented. They fall somewhere between the abstract and figurative pictogram in terms of their representation.

Figure 9-11: A schematic pictogram

the challenge of icons

CREATING A SUCCESSFUL icon requires consideration of multiple factors. For example, because yellow is so visible, the United States and Japan use yellow as a background for road signs that warn of danger. You might expect that all nations would use yellow in their cautionary road signs. They don't. In Europe, road signs warning of danger are outlined in a thick red line.

Hence icon designers face a hurdle when creating an icon: The need to communicate with people from various cultures. Seen in airports, hospitals,

Figure 9-12: A pair of universal icons. Or are they?

stadiums, and theaters throughout the United States, the icons shown in Figure 9-12 indicate the location of restrooms for both men and women. What could be simpler than that? Well, in many cultures, women do not wear skirts. Will a woman from those cultures recognize herself in Figure 9-12?

Icons must also communicate effectively with the vision impaired. Users suffering only from color blindness may find some icons more difficult to interpret.

combining icons with text

OF COURSE, icons and words are not mortal enemies. Some signs combine both, as shown in Figure 9-13, in an effort to ensure that the reader absolutely understands the sign's serious message. Even a stop sign, instantly recognizable by all drivers, still emphasizes its message in a word: STOP.

Figure 9-13: Combining icon and text to communicate a serious message

Particularly in the area of providing help to users, software and hardware manufacturers add icons to allow readers to more easily jump from topic to topic. In Figure 9-14, for example, a page of an online help manual instructs the reader how to troubleshoot a problem with a network printer.

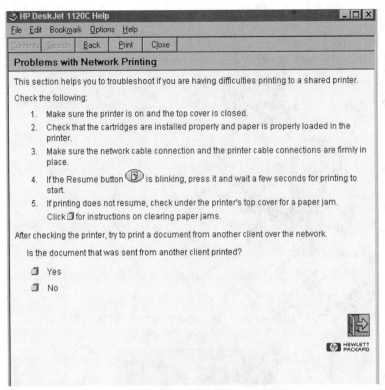

Figure 9-14: This online help manual incorporates several icons
Source: Hewlitt-Packard Company.
Copyright © 2002 Hewlitt-Packard Company. Reproduced with permission.

The page of instructions in Figure 9-14 includes several icons. The first icon represents the printer's *Resume* button, within instructions for using the button. Clicking on the second, third, and fourth icons will take the user to a specific, supplemental page if the icon is clicked. The final icon, in the lower right corner, above the company logo, takes the user to another part of the help manual.

graphs in everyday computer life

ICONS ARE NOT the only forms of visual communication to help us communicate with our PCs or help our PCs communicate with us. *Norton System Works 2001* builds a 3-D column chart to compare the processing speed of the computer being tested with three other personal computer systems, as shown in Figure 9-15. *Windows 98* exhibits a pie chart to establish how much free space is on the hard disk as shown in Figure 9-16.

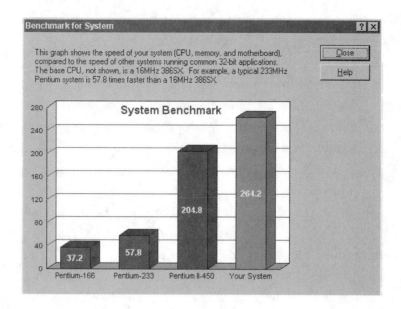

Figure 9-15: This application creates a 3-D column chart to compare the speed of computers

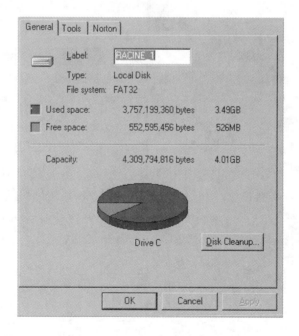

Figure 9-16: *Windows 98* creates a pie chart to compare the amount of free and used disk space

structure of a sample website

HERE IS A FINAL example of how visual communication helps you navigate the world of computers by helping designers and programmers create the Internet world you visit. Early in the development of a website, the website creators describe how visitors will travel through the site. Although several methods are used to do this, Figure 9-17 exemplifies a common form of expressing this information.

This method, however, is somewhat misleading. Actually, lines should be connecting all the rectangles because a visitor to a website can visit any part of the site in any order. Designers do not usually show that level of interconnectivity, to simplify the chart's clarity. Notice also that the chart in Figure 9-17 highlights selected rectangles with different fills and borders to indicate which phase will include creation of that part of the site.

Did you notice the legend in Figure 9-17? Does Figure 9-17 remind you of another form of visual communication?

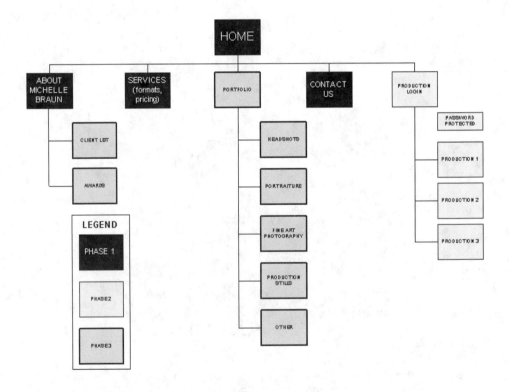

Figure 9-17: A common method for planning construction of a website

binary—a number system with only two numbers: 1 and 0; the only language computers understand

graphical user interface (GUI)—a method of interacting with a personal computer that relies on color buttons, menus, and boxes and a mouse to click on them

icon—within graphic user interfaces, a small graphic image that represents a function the user can manipulate

pane—a frame within a computer screen's window

personal computer (PC)—a computer generally used by a single operator; a computer complete with keyboard and monitor, its own operating system (whether Macintosh or *Windows*), and the ability to use a variety of software applications

personal data assistant (PDA)—a hand-sized personal computer storing telephone numbers, addresses, etc.

pictograms—drawn or painted images that stand for a word or phrase

root folder—the only folder that branches directly from a drive (e.g., c); all other folders branch from the root folder

semiotics—the study of icons and symbols throughout recorded time

subfolder—a folder that branches off from a folder

toolbar—a collection of icons, usually appearing as a single horizontal bar

Ten Traits of a Successful Icon

1. An icon is the best way to present the information or function.
2. The objects in the icon are familiar to the viewer.
3. The image spontaneously suggests the depicted concept to the viewer.
4. The icon uses only those lines, shapes, and colors that are absolutely necessary.
5. A variety of viewers feel a strong connection between the image and the concept.
6. The image communicates what clicking the icon will accomplish for the viewer.
7. The image is striking and memorable.
8. The image appears as a unified graphic, rather than a collection of lines, shapes, and colors.
9. The image communicates why the concept is important.
10. The image remains legible under less-than-ideal viewing conditions.

▶▶▶ learning on your own

1. How many forms of visual communication shown in this chapter were introduced in previous chapters?

2. Based on what you have learned in this chapter, why would structure C in Figure 9-4 on page 183 eventually become a problem?

3. Using icons, not menus (whenever possible), count how many icons you press or click on when you:

   ▸ Turn on your PC
   ▸ Enter your e-mail or word processing application
   ▸ Retrieve, delete, answer, and file e-mails

4. Why do you think the PDA in Figure 9-8 on page 188 repeated several unlabeled icons on its screen? Why do you think the unlabeled icons were labeled on the screen?

chapter
ten

Reaching Your Audience

▶ **Presentation**

▶ *Microsoft PowerPoint*

▶ **Body language**

▶ **Slide**

▶ **Transition**

▶ **Animation**

▶ **Handouts**

overcoming fear

YEAR AFTER YEAR, a polling organization in the United States releases results from its annual effort to discover what Americans fear most. Holding the first or second position each year remains "speaking before a group of people." The poll does not specifically address giving a presentation before a group of people, but that activity would probably rank high on the list.

Even if giving a presentation would be high on your fear list, be forewarned that you may not be able to duck a presentation assignment in your future.

More organizations have committed to creating high-impact presentations as the cost of equipment continues to drop, even adding special rooms dedicated to giving presentations. Laptop computers, with their multimedia capacity, have put the power of sophisticated presentations into the hands of workers in the field. Many organizations now create presentations for in-house quality control and training efforts, not only for external audiences.

Chapter 10 explores how visual communication can make your presentations more effective and more successful. In offering strategies for building a presentation, Chapter 10 incorporates the forms of visual communication you studied in earlier chapters. If you are beginning *Visual Communication* with Chapter 10—hopefully, not the morning before you give a presentation—you will have the chance to explore basic concepts of visual communication.

In keeping with the theme of *Visual Communication*, Chapter 10 focuses on the visual aspects of multimedia presentations. A **multimedia** presentation uses multiple avenues (sight, music, sound, speech) to touch several human senses at once. Although sound (music, recorded narration, sound effects) contributes a key element of multimedia presentations, and presentation applications can embed audio files in their files, this chapter will not discuss that medium, except for a brief discussion of the human voice.

Chapter 10 offers guidelines for creating an effective presentation, no matter the process or equipment you use. The emphasis is on electronic multimedia presentations; however, presenters using whiteboards, easels, or chalkboards face many of the same obstacles when communicating with an audience. Overcoming these obstacles begins with a knowledgeable presenter, able and eager to connect with an audience on a personal level. How important is that connection?

One study of interpersonal communication, conducted by Dr. Albert Mehrabian at the University of California, discovered that the words spoken (verbal) account for only seven percent of the impact of face-to-face communication. Voice characteristics (tone and inflection) account for 38 percent (vocal), and visual communication (frowns, smiles, gestures) account for 55 percent of the impact (visual). Figure 10-1 displays this information in a pie chart.

Components of Face-to-Face Communication and Their Impact (Percent)

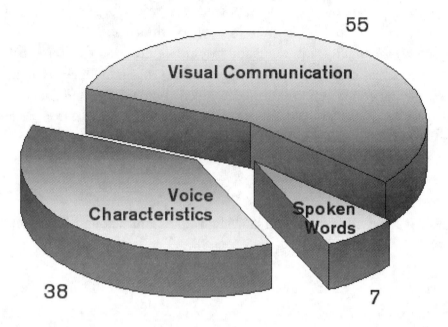

55

Visual Communication

Voice
Characteristics

Spoken
Words

38

7

Figure 10-1: Spoken words have the least impact in fact-to-face communication.

why give a presentation?

FIRST, WE WILL begin with four frequently asked questions about presentations:

- What is a presentation anyway?
- What is the benefit of having an individual share information with a group of people?
- Why not simply distribute a memo?
- When is a presentation appropriate?

what is a presentation anyway?

A **presentation** is an individual speaking to a group for the purpose of exchanging information of common interest. Nothing more. The use of video projectors, *Microsoft PowerPoint,* and sophisticated sound systems has not changed the basic dynamics of a presentation: One individual speaking to a group of individuals. Of course, some meetings (e.g., meetings of company managers or annual stockholder meetings) will feature a series of presenters speaking to an audience, but even in this instance, a single individual usually speaks to the audience at one time.

what is the benefit of having an individual share information with a group of people?

Having an individual stand before an audience to share information has several benefits:

- The presenter shares the same information with the entire audience at the same time. This may significantly reduce the misunderstandings that result from multiple readers drawing their own conclusions while individually reading a document.
- The audience will probably take away some information about the issue presented. In contrast, you cannot depend on everyone reading what you distribute or even skimming it well.
- The audience has an opportunity to question the presenter. (How recent is the data used to create this chart? Can you explain the difference between slide three and slide six? Are you saying our productivity falls as our quality rises?) The audience's opportunity to interact with the presenter marks a key difference between a presentation and a lecture.
- The presenter may use multimedia tools to retain his audience's attention and illustrate his point: Using transitions, one slide can dissolve into another; slides can appear to add elements each time the presenter clicks her mouse button; a skilled presenter can infuse the presentation with movement.

- The presenter has pruned and summarized the information so that she brings only the most vital information to the presentation.
- The presenter controls the order in which her audience absorbs information, placing the points she believes are most significant where they will help the argument the most.
- The presentation can invoke the audience's emotions.
- The presentation can be slightly altered and used for another purpose, reducing the cost of a second presentation.

why not simply distribute a memo?

Realistically, communicating useful information during a presentation remains anything but automatic. The presenter may be so nervous, his material so poorly conceived, his visual communication so complex or difficult to understand, that audience members mumble, "That was a waste of time" as soon as they are out of earshot. Little would be gained from that investment of time. In that case, sending a memo might be just as effective as giving a presentation.

when is a presentation appropriate?

A presentation may be appropriate for several reasons:

- *The presentation contains data so confidential that distributing e-mails or memorandums would be risky.* A business considering a merger, acquisition, bankruptcy, or significant public announcement might very well find itself in this situation.
- *The presenter seeks input from the audience.* He may want suggestions to solve a problem. The presentation may be a draft of a presentation to be presented to another group later. Giving a draft presentation often occurs when the audience of the final presentation is particularly important (e.g., a Board of Directors or corporate creditors) or the content of the presentation has especially meaningful import for an organization (e.g., charitable contributions have fallen).

- *A presentation's multimedia capabilities will be exploited.* Using a presentation to display a series of color photographs, an organization's new logo, or a model of the corporate office's new work area may be more economical than designing and printing hard-copy versions of the information.

Figure 10-2 illustrates why engaging several senses, a strength of multimedia presentations, increases an audience's retention of information.

- *Giving a presentation has value in itself.* A company president might appear before staff members to stifle rumors. A new department manager might give a presentation to introduce himself and his plans for the coming years. A sales representative might use a presentation as a reason to gather a prospective client's decision makers in a room and monopolize their attention.
- *A presentation repeats the information each time.* A manager of a public relations department might prefer that her representatives have a standard, approved presentation describing their organization when they appear before groups.

Retention Rates for Three Ways of Absorbing Information

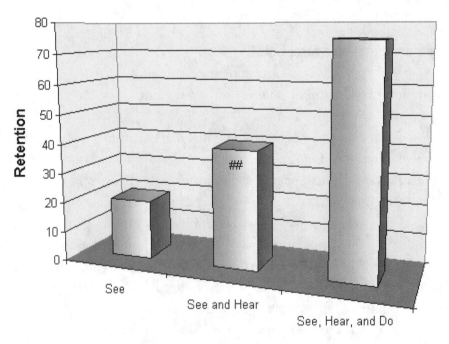

Figure 10-2: Engaging more than one sense increases your audience's retention of information

what to say?

ROBERT L. LINDSTROM, author of the *Business Week Guide to Multimedia Presentations*, has four simple rules of good multimedia presentation:

1. Have something to say.
2. Say it clearly.
3. Say it like you mean it.
4. No amount of technology can help you with Rule #1.

Here is another technique for selecting what to say: Focus on what you want to sell. Let everything else you present support that single goal. When faced with removing a graphic or adding more text, ask yourself a single question: How does this action impact my chances of selling what I want to sell?

You have probably guessed that the paragraph above is targeted to more than salespeople. Every person who gives a presentation is trying to sell *something*. If the person giving the presentation cannot pinpoint what he is selling, he should probably cancel the presentation.

Of course, what you are selling in your presentation may not be a product. It may be an idea, a concept, a new way of doing business, including:

- Convincing management that your department deserves responsibility for creating a new product
- Convincing your supervisor that you need another support person
- Persuading your audience that increased cash flow does allow for an expansion of the manufacturing facility
- Persuading new employees to seek answers from the Human Resources department's new website

Or you may, indeed, be persuading a potential client that your product or service is the best fit for her needs.

Did you notice that the bulleted items immediately above all begin with *convincing* or *persuading*? Those are the requirements you must meet before you reach your goal. You must persuade and convince your audience so they will buy what you are selling. Creating a dozen lovely charts or 60 striking *PowerPoint* slides will fall flat without the requisite persuasive aspect. Audiences don't act because of information. They act because you persuaded them that the action you suggest is the best action for them. After all, you are asking them to do something. This something might cost money, involve a risk, cause upheaval, or change they way they run their business or live their lives.

the power of the presenter

IF YOU HAVE worked in an organization for a while, you have probably been a victim of a "going-through-the-motions" presenter. The *going-through-the-motions* presenter probably:

- Is bored
- Believes the presentation is stealing time from his real work
- Believes the material should be obvious to everyone
- Believes the audience has little valuable to add to his understanding or communication of his data
- Considers the explaining of the presentation's material beneath him. (Sometimes this manner actually results from the presenter being afraid of speaking before an audience.)

> **Visual communication extends to body language—such as hand movement, body position, and facial expression—all are tools of commentary and emphasis.**

The *going-through-the-motions* presenter usually falls into a combination of these traps:

- Ignores her audience
- Speaks in a monotone
- Shows no emotion or excitement
- Rarely, if ever, smiles
- Stands with her back to the audience (facing the presentation)
- Never moves from a single spot on the floor

> Whether you dread giving presentations or look forward to giving them, you probably experience a rush of excitement when you begin speaking. Avoid allowing this rush of excitement to spur you to speak faster. Listen to yourself during the course of the presentation. You don't want to lose your audience's attention because you speak too quickly.

Whatever the presenter's reason for being less than dynamic, the audience begins to feel the presenter would rather be somewhere else. And soon, so do they.

> Keep your face—a great tool of communication—toward the audience. If you must walk to the projected image of your slide, do not turn your back to your audience. Instead, walk backward.

the power of the audience

IF YOUR ONLY goal is to dump a vast amount of information on an audience and then thank them for their attention before you exit, then your audience has little power. If you want that audience to act, however, the audience has a hold over you. Why? Because the audience can frustrate your goals by doing nothing. They may not complain about your presentation technique or question your supporting evidence.

Perhaps that is why businesspeople must sit through so many *going-through-the-motions* presentations: Most presenters have forgotten they need to win action from their audience. A good start is understanding the composition and motivations of your audience. Figure 10-3 offers questions to help you focus on exactly that.

Step	Question
1.	What do you want from your audience?
2.	What is the average age of your audience?
3.	What is the mix of genders in your audience?
4.	What is audience's level of expertise?
5.	What will most persuade your audience? ▶ Multimedia? ▶ Charts? ▶ Brief pieces of text?
6.	What has the audience done just before this presentation, or what will it do immediately after your presentation? ▶ Arrive at work ▶ Finish lunch ▶ Leave for home

Figure 10-3: Key questions to understanding your audience

The answers to these questions will shape your presentation. For example, if your presentation falls immediately after lunch (a presenter's nightmare), you will have to begin your presentation with a flourish, including aggressively connecting with your audience.

> Avoid falling into the trap of using ALL CAPITAL LETTERS for emphasis. Placing more than seven consecutive words in all capital letters will force your audience to read the words again—if they read the words at all.

about *Microsoft PowerPoint*

MICROSOFT POWERPOINT REMAINS the most popular presentation application for *Windows*. The following section offers an introduction to *PowerPoint XP* (*PowerPoint 2002*), the latest version of *PowerPoint*.

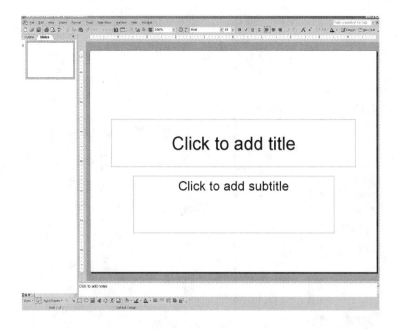

Figure 10-4: *PowerPoint XP*'s opening screen

Based on the metaphor of a 35mm transparency or slide, once the cutting edge technology for creating presentations, *PowerPoint* presents the user with a landscape, a rectangular working area named a **slide**, as shown in Figure 10-4. By creating a series of slides, the user creates a presentation.

PowerPoint strives to make creating presentations easy, and the application has enabled workers with no graphics or visual communication training to produce visually pleasing presentations. To help users (particularly users new to *PowerPoint*) start quickly, *PowerPoint* offers several options. Users can:

- Edit a presentation that already exists
- Choose the *Auto Content Wizard*, which walks you through a series of questions to customize a common presentation type
- Begin a presentation by completing an outline
- Open a content layout, a simple way to add clip art or media clips to a presentation
- Begin with a blank presentation, after which you can add all the text and graphics yourself
- Select a design template, which applies a design to every slide in your presentation (the left image in Figure 10-5 displays multiple design templates)

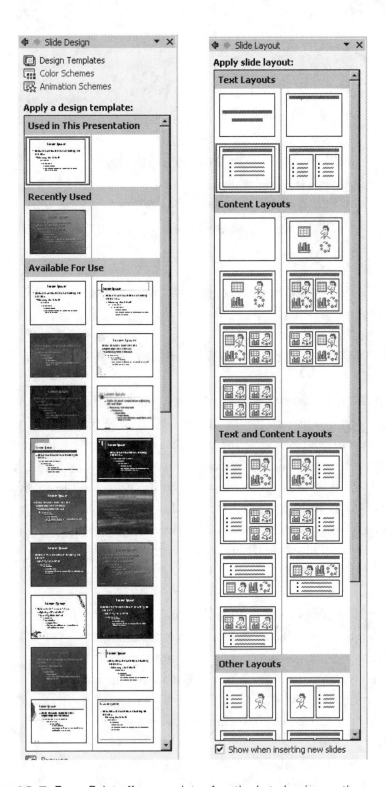

Figure 10-5: PowerPoint offers a variety of methods to begin creating a presentation

what kind of presentation do you need?

POWER POINT SERVES up an array of elements to insert in your presentation, including visual images from video to animated text. Before you insert too many images into your presentation, start with several questions designed to get your feet planted on firm ground.

- How long will your presentation be?
- What medium will be used? (*PowerPoint*? Whiteboard? Flip Chart?)
- How many graphics will be needed?
- What message must each piece of graphics communicate?
- What text *must* be covered?
- Will you have the equipment to present a multimedia presentation?
- Is a multimedia presentation appropriate?

Just as it accepts word processing tables, *PowerPoint* allows users of spreadsheet programs to paste charts directly onto slides. *PowerPoint* also has simplified applications for creating its own charts, diagrams, flowcharts, organization charts, and tables.

In following sections, you will see some of the strengths of *PowerPoint*, as well as cautions about the limitations of presentations and examples of poorly design slides.

A *PowerPoint* presentation, in combination with a video projector, offers three major advantages over other forms of presentation:

- Incorporation of multimedia
- Transitions
- Animations

As you construct your presentation, periodically test it in the environment in which it will be given. If you will give your presentation with a video projector in a long, thin room, test the presentation there—well before the time of the actual presentation. During the test, walk through the room, checking that audience members sitting in the back and on the outside aisles are able to see your work.

Transitions are visual effects *between* slides; rather than having one slide disappear and another replace it, a transition can be added between slides, so that one slide appears to dissolve into another. *PowerPoint XP* offers 58 transition styles to connect individual slides or entire presentations.

Animations are visual effects *within* slides. For example, titles bounce into their proper place on slides or bulleted lists gradually appear on the slides and then unzip to their full length. Similar to transitions, animations can be added to selected slides or entire presentations. *PowerPoint XP* includes 33 animation styles.

why include transitions and animations?

SIMPLY PUT, your audience thinks more of you when your presentation includes these techniques. A study by the Management Information Systems Department of the University of Arizona, compared the impact of presentations containing no visual content to presentations containing transitions and animations. Figure 10-6 illustrates how the audience's perception of the presenter increased when animations and transitions were used onscreen.

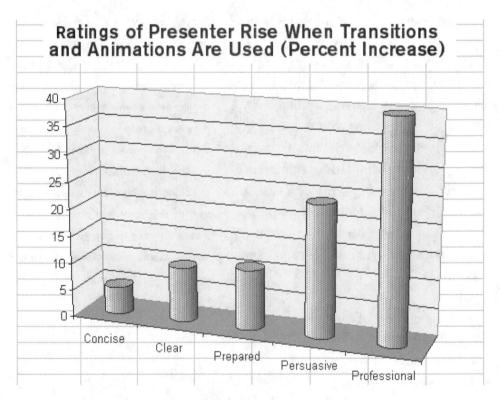

Figure 10-6: Transitions and animations increase an audience's perception of a presenter

If you introduce transitions into your presentation, use the same style of transition throughout the presentation. This gives you the *wow* of transitions without jarring the audience or distracting them from your message. And because you include transitions between some slides, doesn't mean you need to insert transitions between *all* slides. Save your bag of tricks for the crucial slides and the major concepts they contain.

all colors are not created equal

AS MENTIONED IN Chapter 1, colors help you gain and hold attention in an information-saturated world. Highlighting crucial information in color, for instance, helps your audience focus on that information. Selecting a set of colors to appear on each slide sets a tone for the presentation.

Some colors behave differently in a presentation, however, depending how they are placed. For example:

- Colored objects on a white background appear smaller
- Colored objects on a black background appear larger

Color can also differentiate elements of a slide, helping an audience follow your format. You might format each slide title in blue, for example, and each block of body text in green. Remember to select the same color for each element throughout your presentation or you will confuse your audience.

Sara Stohl, an expert in the design of presentations that communicate technical data, believes colors communicate a distinct message to audiences. Figure 10-7 presents some of these messages. As you can surmise, colors are valuable tools for gaining an emotional response from your audience.

Twenty percent of human males have some difficulty distinguishing between blue and yellow or red and green.

Color	Characteristic
Black	Forceful, stubborn, direct, extinct
Blue	Conservative, relaxing, fulfillment, loyalty, secure
Brown	Sincerity, corporate authority, dullness
Gray	Noncommittal, secrecy, neutral, reserved
Green	Intelligence, suggestion, development, hopeful, growth
Purple	Enchantment, immaturity, insecurity
Red	Desire, passion, fire, danger, power, competition
White	Pure, blankness, basic
Yellow	Excitement, attention, emphasis, special, bright

Figure 10-7: General characteristics of colors and their interpretation by audiences

more detail doesn't equal better

PRESUMABLY, YOU HAVE been asked to give a presentation because you know a great deal about the subject matter being presented. Being an expert, however, leads to the temptation to elaborate and present great detail on your subject. Sometimes, that temptation should be resisted. Figure 10-8 is a slide describing Grainville Baking Company's new accounting system. Clearly, there is too much information on this slide. Even for an audience familiar with accounting, Figure 10-8 features a number of convoluted arrows and tiny text (*Integrated, Manual*).

Not all information fits the presentation slide format. Omitting extraneous detail makes your presentation leaner, faster, and more focused.

> Each presentation should have a "wow" factor. A *wow* graphic or animation contains such high visual interest that it keeps an audience alert and demonstrates your competency. Too many *wow* elements, however, detract from your basic goal: To sell your audience what you want to sell them.

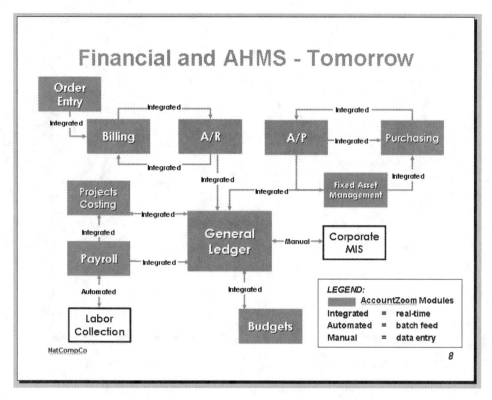

Figure 10-8: A complex flowchart requiring considerable explanation

conserving onscreen real estate

SOME PRESENTERS SEEM to feel insecure if they don't fill each slide edge to edge with words or graphics. You will escape that mistake if you remember that even an attentive audience deserves a rest. A slide with plenty of empty space (referred to as **white space** or **negative space**) allows a brief rest from the previous piece of information. After all, considering and responding to information—exactly what you want your audience to do—takes energy and concentration. Presentation applications offer you, the presentation designer, many templates with attractive backgrounds. Allow your audience to see those backgrounds periodically.

Figure 10-9 contains a slide with so much information, an audience must struggle to absorb it all. Notice how close the company name (lower left corner) and slide number (lower right corner) are to the data, a clue that the table is too large for the slide.

Cost Incurred

	February YTD			Variance		
	Actual	Plan	Variance	SMS	ERP	Bus Sol
Direct Labor	10,127	11,652	1,525	1,166	161	197
ODC	20,273	18,893	(1,380)	(596)	(261)	(522)
Total Direct	30,400	30,545	145	570	(100)	(325)
Indirect Expenses						
Indirect Labor	5,493	4,816	(677)	(93)	(594)	10
Office Expenses	263	180	(83)	(73)	(2)	(8)
Software Purchases	19	42	23	23	-	-
Repair & Maintenance (Utilities)	528	570	42	-	56	(14)
Equipment Leased	34	9	(25)	(25)	-	-
Equipment Purchased	258	166	(92)	(28)	(68)	4
Depreciation/Amortization	397	324	(73)	(60)	(15)	2
Outside Services	177	129	(48)	(24)	(21)	(3)
Transportation	750	648	(102)	13	(139)	24
Education & Training	-	112	112	-	112	-
Tax & Business Fees	29	11	(18)	-	(27)	9
Other	21	193	172	139	(7)	40
Total Indirect Expenses	7,969	7,200	(769)	(128)	(705)	64
Total LOB Direct and Indirect	38,369	37,745	(624)	442	(805)	(261)
Infrastructure Cost	444	726	282	282	-	-
Total Cost of Goods Sold	38,813	38,471	(342)	724	(805)	(261)

NatCompCo 3

Figure 10-9: A table more appropriate to a report than a presentation

When you create your own presentations, remember that you are giving an overview, not a report. The *PowerPoint* slides appearing behind you *augment* your communication. They are not your communication.

When selecting a location for your presentation, consider the position of doors and windows. If you will be presenting during daylight, project your image away from windows to reduce glare. Similarly, project your image at a distance from doors. Someone always enters a presentation late or leaves early, distracting your audience.

placing content

KEEP THESE SUGGESTIONS in mind as you lay out your slides:

- Restrict each slide to presenting one concept per slide.
- Choose concise statements throughout; complete sentences are not required.
- Limit yourself to no more than eight lines of text per slide. Remember, you can always flow any remaining text to the next slide.
- Limit your lines of text to no more than eight words per line.
- Include verbs as much as possible. Verbs generally reduce a reliance on passive voice and bring action to your text. Some presentation consultants even recommend beginning each line of text with a verb.

staying within the lines

CONSIDER THESE TWO guidelines when designing the layout of your presentation.

1. Place the title of each slide in the same position. Move the title slightly if you need an extra bit of space for a terrific graphic, but if you find yourself moving the title a significant amount, you have too much content on that slide. Figure 10-10 displays a new PowerPoint slide, complete with suggested guidelines for the title and text block.
2. Decide on consistent placement for text blocks. Will the text be centered on each slide? Flush left? Flush right?

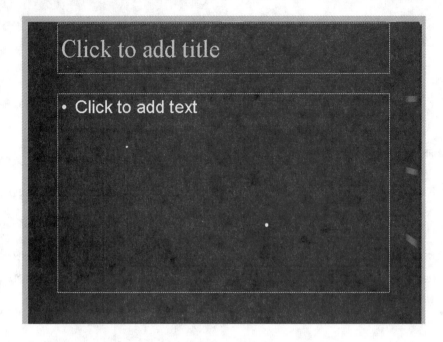

Figure 10-10: A new *PowerPoint* slide includes guidelines
for the size of a title and text block

Would you like to show your presentation to someone who doesn't
own *PowerPoint*? You can do exactly that. *PowerPoint's Pack and Go*
function allows you to send *PowerPoint Viewer* with a presentation,
so anyone can review your *PowerPoint* presentation on his or her PC.
Your reviewer cannot edit the presentation—which you wouldn't want
anyway—but he can view the presentation just as you created it.

to hand out or not to hand out

POWERPOINT PRODUCES more than presentations. The application also
prints accurate hard-copy versions of its presentations, in either color or black
and white. In fact, some organizations use *PowerPoint* to produce documents
such as proposals and reports. The most common use of *PowerPoint's* printing
capability, however, centers on the printing of handouts. **Handouts** capture
one or more slides on a sheet of paper and are frequently distributed to an audience for reinforcement of a presentation.

Whether you want to distribute handouts depends on your goals and preferences as a presenter. Figure 10-11 delineates the pros and cons of handouts.

Pros	Cons
Allows the audience to review the presentation later.	▸ Distracts the audience from the presentation.
	▸ May compromise confidentiality.
	▸ May entice presenter to include complex graphs and tables unsuitable for a presentation.
Allows the audience to review complex concepts during presentation.	▸ Presenter should have sumrized and explained complex concepts.
Allows audience members in the back to follow the presentation, even if they cannot see the slide.	▸ May require some lights to be on so audience members can read the handout.
	▸ Lights often detract from presentation colors.
Allows those not at the presentation to review the material at their convenience.	▸ Reduces presentation to just another document, eliminating the impact of multimedia.
	▸ Lacks additional matter discussed or questions answered.

Figure 10-11: Arguments for and against distributing handouts

size matters

AUDIENCES APPRECIATE CONSISTENCY. Consistency makes their job easier. They know that significant items are formatted in larger type, just as the major points on a bulleted list are marked with larger bullets than a sublist.

Shrinking type size to squeeze in more text or an oversized graphic sacrifices consistency and confounds your audience. If you must shrink the size of text, never shrink it more than four points from its original size. For instance, if *PowerPoint* formats text at 24 points, do not reduce the type size to less than 20 points. (If you begin typing in a *PowerPoint* text box, you can discover *PowerPoint's* suggested type size by checking the *Font Size* icon on the *PowerPoint* toolbar.)

A measurement common in the desktop publishing and printing worlds, **points** are used to measure the height of type. One point equals $\frac{1}{72}$ of an inch.

What is the smallest type size you can use in a presentation that your audience can read? Decide that question yourself with this simple test. On the floor, place a printout of a slide from your presentation with the text formatted in the smallest type size. From a standing position, if you can read the text (no fair bending over), the type is large enough for your audience. Figure 10-12 illustrates what happens when the type size is sacrificed.

Once again, in the interest of consistency, use no more than two type sizes throughout a presentation (excluding headings).

Figure 10-12: The amount of data within this slide requires diminished text size

If you are going to give a presentation using only the monitor on your computer, without projecting the image, limit your audience to no more than ten people; even a large monitor fails to provide enough clear sight lines for an audience bigger than that.

the greatest factor

EVEN THE MOST appealing form of visual communication loses its power if an audience has seen it a dozen times. Audiences grow jaded. Your ability to explain to an audience, to listen to them, to sense their confusion or their excitement remains the single greatest factor in a successful presentation. If your audience leaves your presentation a little more inspired, informed, concerned, or thoughtful, you have succeeded. If they don't, you have failed—no matter how many pieces of electronics surround you.

Meeting this high standard isn't easy. If it were, everyone would be doing it well.

GLOSSARY

animations—**visual effects within slides in an electronic presentation**

body language—**gesture, body position, and facial expression**

handouts—**hard copies that capture one or more slides on a sheet of paper and are frequently distributed to an audience for a presentation**

multimedia—**using multiple avenues of media to affect several senses**

point—**a unit of typographical measurement (of the height of the type or line space); one point equals $\frac{1}{72}$ of an inch**

presentation—**an individual or individuals speaking before a group for the purpose of exchanging information of common interest**

slide—**a landscape, rectangular working area, equivalent to a page in a word processing document**

transitions—**visual effects between slides in an electronic presentation**

white space (negative space)—**empty space surrounding a graphic or text**

Ten Tips for Improving Your Presentations

The more you invest in a presentation, the more confident you will be when you give the presentation. As you grow more confident giving presentations, the more likely you will be asked to give them, which should offer you an opportunity to invest yourself in another presentation. See a pattern here? Incorporating the following tips will improve your presentations and reduce your nervousness while giving them.

	Action	Explanation
1.	Assume the audience has no clue what you want.	As you build your presentation, it is so easy to learn the presentation *too well*. Preview your work to a person you trust, someone who knows nothing about the points you want to make.
2.	Set a deadline and stick to it.	This may be the most difficult action in this list. If you have others contributing to your presentation, you will need to be especially firm. You will need a deadline so that people, including you, will stop revising. In addition, you cannot have a final rehearsal if material continues streaming into the presentation.
3.	Rehearse.	Yes, you're busy. Think how busy you will be if you have to give a second presentation to explain the first presentation. Do you know where all the transitions occur in your presentation? A thorough rehearsal will show you. For an important presentation, rehearse the presentation three times, including all the transitions, animations, and sound cues.

4.	Be ready when the first audience members arrive.	This gives you the chance to greet individual audience members as they arrive. Also, if you have rehearsed and checked all the equipment before the audience arrives, you have a great shot at beginning the presentation calmly and surely. You also communicate to the audience that you are prepared, even before the first slide appears on screen.
5.	Use your arms to good effect.	Do you tend to cross your arms across your chest? Some see that motion as signifying you are closed to new ideas. Do you flap your hands or arms when you are speaking or nervous? Be aware of the position of your arms and the speed at which you are moving them.
6.	Allow pauses.	Do not talk nonstop during a presentation. For example, don't talk over a sound clip. Allow a several-second pause between particularly important slides or graphics. Remember, your audience may be absorbing your last point or taking notes.
7.	Project your voice to the back of the room.	The audience member farthest from your voice deserves to hear you. Don't trust the sound system you are using. Ask the audience members farthest from your voice if they can hear you.
8.	Make eye contact.	Avoid staring at your equipment or screen, as if you expected them to fail at any moment. Instead, glance from audience member to audience member to check that you are engaging them.
9.	Ask for questions as if you really want questions.	Questions from the audience create an opportunity for you to make a point you forgot or elaborate on a key concept. A question from one audience member might represent the thoughts of a dozen audience members.
10.	Move around the room.	This doesn't mean to pace back and forth between two distinct points like a human wiper blade. Try walking into the audience while you elaborate on a slide or a question from the audience.

▶▶ learning on your own

1. Design a presentation on a special interest project or a hobby using a flash card for each screen.

2. In light of what you've learned in this chapter, critique your presentation. Then make two lists:
   - What you did well
   - What you can improve upon

3. Leaf through a magazine or newspaper, and find a graphic that would be
   - Ideal for a *PowerPoint* presentation
   - All wrong for a *PowerPoint* presentation
   - Support your choices with reasoning.

appendix

Online and Print Resources

listed here are publications and websites that contain entertaining and relevant information on the different topics discussed in *Visual Communication*. At time of publication, all websites listed here were active, but due to the ever-changing climate of the Internet, we cannot guarantee every link will be current.

websites

- Some history of visual literacy:
  www.asu.edu/lib/archives/vlhist.htm
- Pomona College's Online Visual Literacy Project:
  www.pomona.edu/Academics/courserelated/classprojects/Visual-lit/
  intro/intro.html
- A good resource site; includes references to books about Gantt charts and
  project management:
  www.smartdraw.com
- An interactive online tutorial for Spatial Intelligence:
  www.ul.ie/~mearsa/9519211/
- Online multiple intelligence tests for kids, youths, and adults:
  www.dwci.edu/facstaff/~csauer/Links/Tests/tests.htm
- Introductory explanations of PERT and Gantt charts:
  http://studentweb.tulane.edu/%7Emtruill/dev-pert.html
- Site that shows visitors how to draw landscape maps:
  www.learn2.com/09/0930/09302.asp
- Interesting icon gallery:
  www.thecorporation.com/icon/gallery1.html
- Excellent source for Web graphics:
  www.gograph.com
- The CIA's online *World Factbook 2001*:
  www.cia.gov/cia/publications/factbook/
- The National Atlas on the Internet:
  www.nationalatlas.gov

books

Coe, Marlana. *Human Factors* (New York: Wiley, 1996).

Smit, Kornelis and Howard Chandler. *Means Illustrated Construction Dictionary*. 3d ed. (Kingston, MA: Robert S. Means, 1991).

Weaver, Marcia. *Visual Literacy: How to Read and Use Information in the Graphic Form* (New York: LearningExpress, 1999).

Wildbur, Peter and Michael Burke. *Information Graphics* (London: Thames and Hudson, 1998).

Wilde, Judith and Richard Wilde. *Visual Literacy: A Conceptual Approach to Graphic Problem Solving* (Watson-Guptill: 2000).

Zelansky, Gene. *Say It with Charts: The Executive's Guide to Visual Communication* (New York: McGraw-Hill, 2001).